GODSEND

MICHAEL MOYNAGH

Published by Fresh Expressions Limited 2021
freshexpressions.org.uk
fxresourcing.org

CONTENTS

OVERVIEW

1. LOVE

WHERE IT ALL STARTS

Imagine that God has plans for the universe and is inviting you to get involved. How could you join in when you're not sure how your faith relates to your everyday life? Or when your week is crowded out with so many things already?

Godsend is a life-centred, 21st century way of following Jesus.

First, you find a friend or two. Then together you find simple ways to love the people round you – in your neighbourhood, your workplace, or as you're doing something you really enjoy.

You make friends with the people involved, share your faith, and a new Christian community emerges where you are.

Your new community doesn't stand alone. It might be connected to an existing congregation or a regional grouping of churches. If you like, you can think of it as a new congregation or a new Christian community within your local church.

Maybe the idea sounds a bit daunting, but this overview shows you how simple it can be. The rest of Godsend explores the detail.

This is a book version of the FX Godsend app. The chapters integrate the Animation, Guide and an abbreviated version of Action in each of the main units.

The big theme is love. How can Christians show love in their everyday lives in a 21st century way?

1. FIRST STEP: FOLLOW JESUS WITH SOMEONE

Find a friend (or more!) in your workplace, family, circle of acquaintances, passion, neighborhood, or where you spend much of your time.

A young man passed a small building site walking to work. He decided to give workers there free donuts once a week, as an expression of Christian love.

The first few times went well. But then he stopped.

Keeping it up week after week without a friend on the same page felt too difficult. He needed someone with the same vision so that they could support, help and motivate each other.

Following Jesus is difficult when you do it alone. That's why in Luke 10.1 Jesus sent out his disciples in pairs.

So get together with a friend – and ask for God's help.

2. DISCOVER A SIMPLE WAY TO LOVE PEOPLE ROUND YOU...

... and build friendships with them. Here are four examples:

Knit and Natter began when Christine Crowder met with three friends and created an opportunity for people to knit for a purpose. They knitted prayer shawls for the bereaved, blankets for the local women's refuge and hats for shoebox appeals.

And they prayed for the people who would receive them.

Before long, 30 or more people were involved. Most were not attending church. Short devotions at the end proved popular.

Gradually, step-by-step, a new worshipping community has emerged.

Stepping Stones started with some Christians asking how they could lovingly serve families of the local school.

They held parties in the school and beach outings. People got to know each other better and trust grew.

The leaders then offered a course introducing Jesus.

Fit for Life is the strapline of a group in Hampshire, England. Christians connect with people who enjoy running, go to the gym or play football. They have a drink with them afterwards and become friends.

A monthly lunch after Sunday football involves 40 people who are into these health and fitness activities.

Might evenings on spiritual health and fitness be a next step? 'Jesus is one of the world's greatest spiritual coaches. Let's look at his advice and see if we agree.'

Laura gathered teenagers round eating puddings. They shared what was going on for each of them. One of them prayed after each person shared.

Virtually none of them were attending church, but they were learning to follow Jesus together.

3. ENHANCE WHAT YOU'RE DOING

Don't take on an extra commitment unrelated to your passion or interest. Enhance what you are already into – like Louisa.

Louisa was a community nurse in England's East Midlands. She knew that many young mothers locally suffered from post-natal depression.

She chatted to Charlie and his wife who lived near these mothers. Up popped an idea.

The couple would host a weekly drop-in centre for mothers and their children. Louisa would be present with her medical expertise.

After a while, the mothers wanted to meet up on a separate occasion while their partners babysat.

Charlie suggested a menu of things the women might do when they met. They decided to watch a video with stories about lives being changed by God.

So began the journey toward a new Christian community, which enriched the group.

4. THIS WAS NOT A NEW TIME-DEMANDING CHURCH COMMITMENT

Louisa just sowed a spiritual extra into a major part of her life.

It was an exciting way to 'love your neighbour as yourself' (Mark 12.31).

Anyone can do something like this:

- Not just young people
- Nor people from one particular church tradition
- Nor people with a gift of evangelism

Whatever your background, it could be you!

5. NEXT STEPS

Prayerfully

- Find a friend (or more!)
- Explore a simple way to love people you're connected with
- Build friendships with those involved
- Look for natural and appropriate opportunities to share your faith

Worried by the last step? No need to be! The next chapter shows how you can do this almost without knowing!

DISCUSSION

Choose one or more of the following:

READ

Read Matthew 25.14-30. Parable of the talents.

- Imagine this story happened today. What would it look like?
- What 'talents' – interests/passions, gifts/abilities, knowledge/experiences – has God given to you? How might you share them with other people in your network, neighborhood, workplace, or another focus of your life?
- Who could you do this with?

REFLECT

As you have explored this chapter, how have you reacted?

- What's excited you?
- What's challenged you?
- What reservations or questions are you left with?
- In the light of your reactions, which part of Godsend would you like to explore next?

2. SHARE FAITH

EASIER THAN YOU THINK

Why not follow Jesus in a 21st century way?

Find a friend or two in a corner of your life.

Prayerfully discover a simple way to love the people round you.

Make friends with them.

And when the opportunity arises, share stories about your faith as part of helping each other toward a fuller life.

Does that last bit trouble you? If so, don't imagine that you would be trying to persuade people to become Christians. That could feel unnatural, or even unkind if you ended up pressurizing them.

Instead, think of sharing your faith as interpretation. Christians are called to interpret Jesus to other people. Just as an interpreter translates one language into another, Christians translate their faith into the 'language' of the people round them.

You don't need clever arguments. Just talk about what your faith means to you. Let the other person disagree with you and share their own beliefs.

Interpretation is what Jesus did. He interpreted the kingdom of God to people using stories they could understand. People were free to respond however they liked.

We share things that matter to us all the time. You'd tell your friends about a bargain, wouldn't you? So, if Jesus has been good news for you, why not share him too?

Afraid you'll look stupid? Don't worry! Sharing your faith can be as natural as recommending a good hairdresser or telling a friend about a good deal. Here is how.

1. IF YOU ARE INVOLVED IN A MISSION ACTIVITY...

Add a spiritual dimension alongside it.

A weekly luncheon club met at the back of one rural church. Hardly any of the regulars worshiped on Sunday. The leaders invited guests – with no pressure – to gather after lunch around the holy table, which they'd moved into the body of the church.

- They lit a candle
- played some Christian music
- read a story from Scripture
- had some silence
- read one or two prayers
- no more than 15 minutes in all

Almost everyone stayed behind. The beginning of a new congregation?

2. OR PERHAPS YOU ARE STARTING SOMETHING NEW

Issue a welcoming invitation. For example, imagine Jane teams up with Jalal. They give free croissants and decent coffee to their work colleagues each Monday morning. This provokes conversations and strengthens office relationships.

When asked why, they say something like 'We're into practical spirituality, and this is what we do.'

If pressed, they add:

'If you want to know more, we meet after work on Tuesdays and for three quarters of an hour we explore spirituality. Jesus is known as one of the world's greatest spiritual teachers. We look at stories he told and see if we agree with them. Why don't you come and see what we do?'

3. ANYONE COULD DO THIS!

Say Gary accepts the invitation. One of the group photocopies the Bible passage, and explains that they look at the story over several weeks. 'We let it seep into our lives and see what happens.'

They prayerfully read the story and ask, 'If this story happened today, what would it look like?' They have fun re-imagining the story in their context.

Next time they re-read the story, recap their previous discussion and ask, 'What is this story saying to me?' (What am I getting out of it? What's it about?)

In the third week they discuss, 'Could the story make a difference to my life? If so, how?'

Someone explains, 'We've said we're into practical spirituality. So we see if the story does make a difference and report back next time. We are cool about this. It's an experiment. So by definition it might work, it might not. Either way, let's share what happened when we meet again.'

When they next meet, they share their experiences by asking, 'Did the story make a difference? If so, how?'

Here is an easy way to introduce people to Jesus – just four enjoyable questions.

- If this story happened today, what would it look like?
- What is this story saying to me?
- Could the story make difference to my life? How?
- Did the story make a difference? How?

Gary's not embarrassed. It is easy for him to take part. And sharing your Christian faith is simple. Just join in the discussion and answer, 'Did the story make a difference to your life?'

4. DON'T BE AN EXPERT!

Worried that Gary would ask questions you can't answer? Or that he'd find good reasons to disagree with your answers and you'd look stupid?

If so, you don't have to answer people's questions!

If someone asks a factual question and you're not sure of the answer, invite the group to Google it. (After all, this is a 21st century way of following Jesus!) You can discuss which are good sites to visit.

When someone asks a question of opinion, reply: 'From what we know about Jesus so far, what do we think he would say?' Suggest people prayerfully consider their responses, and then share what they think God has said to them (if they believe in him).

Encourage people to listen to, rather than correct each other. Remind them that the church is full of different views, and this diversity can give us a broader glimpse of God.

Keep responding like this and you will teach people the wonderful habit of grounding their thoughts on Christ.

Our eternal destiny does not depend on getting the 'right' answer. We are saved by grace, not right answers! So don't worry about what people say. Far more important is to help them learn the habit of taking their bearings from Jesus.

And especially important is this key principle: you are introducing people to Jesus in a way that leaves room for the Spirit and empowers the explorer.

5. A PATH TO MATURITY

As soon as you can, ask Gary to lead the discussion. Give him the story. He knows the questions. All he needs do is to watch the time, keep the group on task and give everyone a chance to talk – time, task, talk.

When people need more solid food, point one person to a

website with background information about the Bible passage and another to a different website interpreting the story. They share what they've learnt before the discussion. Or discuss a podcast or YouTube video by a recognised Christian authority.

The group is now accessing wisdom from the wider church.

Encourage members to connect with the wider family in other ways – e.g. to join activities with a local congregation or church the community is linked to.

Members come to rely on the Spirit through Scripture, the insights of the group, experience, and the church at large.

Gospel-lite? No way!

6. THIS APPROACH HAS BIG ADVANTAGES

- Anyone can do it
- Enquirers easily join in
- The Bible tells people about Jesus, through the Spirit
- Christians share their faith almost without knowing
- People exploring faith see how the Bible and the Christian family make a difference
- Leadership is shared with newcomers, increasing their commitment to the group
- New Christians learn how to study the Bible on their own, apply it to their lives, share it with their friends, and find helpful resources
- If the leader moves on, the group has the means to keep going – sustainability is built in

To start a new Christian community, you don't need lots of theology, nor to be able to answer difficult questions!

7. JUST TRUST THE SPIRIT!

And – vitally important – respect the other person!

DISCUSSION

Choose one or more of the following:

READ

If you are in a group, try discovery Bible study yourselves. Choose a story about Jesus (or one he told) and prayerfully ask the four questions in the Guide. (You may need to do this over several sessions). Then review your experience.

- Did you enjoy studying the Bible in this way?
- What are the strengths and weaknesses of this approach?
- Can you imagine doing this with people who are exploring the Christian faith? How might you adapt it?

(For some alternative approaches, see Chapter 12.)

IMAGINE

Either as a group or as individuals, select an aspect of your life outside the church that matters to you. Prayerfully imagine that in a dream, prompted by the Spirit, you saw yourself and your Christian friends loving others in a way that really excited people in that context.

- What would be happening to excite people?
- Who would be most excited, and what would they be saying and doing?
- What questions would they ask you?
- How would you frame your reply to include an invitation to explore Jesus?
- How would you help them to explore Jesus – when would you meet? Where? For how long? What would you do?

3. NEW CHRISTIAN COMMUNITY

EXTENDING GOD'S WELCOME

Have you thought about this?

Congregations or churches, whether old or new, are exclusive by their very nature. Once you've decided to meet at a certain time and place, with a particular agenda and style, you'll attract some people, but you're bound to exclude others.

For example:

- If you meet on a Sunday morning, you'll exclude people on shift work and families whose situations make that time impractical
- Where you meet will exclude anyone who can't travel to that place
- If your agenda is to worship Jesus, you'll exclude people who are not interested in him
- And if your worship involves a traditional sermon, anyone who resists being told what to do or think will run a mile!

We meet in an exclusive way, but we worship a God who died on the cross with his arms outstretched in a welcome to everyone. How can we square the circle?

Perhaps the best way is to start new Christian communities with people whom the church currently leaves out.

These communities will meet at different times and places, with different styles and agendas, so they can welcome the many kinds of people who don't fit into existing congregations.

So, imagine you've found a friend, discovered a simple way to love people round you, built friendships with them, and shared your faith.

You know it won't work to invite these "emerging Christians" to an existing church – at least, not yet. The cultural gap between them and church is to wide

1. SO WHAT NEXT?

Form a new Christian community where people are. Meet regularly to:

- discuss the Bible
- pray
- worship

And ask God to help you.

2. INTRODUCING WORSHIP CAN BE EASY

Continue with Discovery Bible Study described in Chapter 3.

Then, for example, light a candle, play some Christian music, let people sing in their hearts, and have a short time of prayerful silence. You don't have to sing or pray out loud.

If you use music, find types of worship music that match the culture of the people you are with.

When you encourage people to pray, why not use a well-chosen scent? Revelation 5.8 likens prayer to incense. Fragrances have long been used in Christian worship.

Encourage gifts within the community. Invite someone:

- · To enrich your worship with photos expressing God's greatness or highlighting issues for prayer
- · To contribute a poem (their own or published)
- · To bring an object they have made, or an object from home that speaks to them
- · To write Christian lyrics to a pop song
- · To bring a prayer they have found or written themselves and read it out (this could be a first step to spoken prayer)

If possible, meet over a meal and include planning in your worship. Mix study, prayer, worship, fellowship and organising.

During the Last Supper, Jesus and his community ate and worshipped together, but also did some planning – 'after my resurrection, meet me in Galilee,' said Jesus (Mark 14.28).

Take worship into life through a WhatsApp group or with Zoom meet-ups. Through the week, community members can "encourage one another daily" (Hebrews 3.13) and share prayer requests, answers to prayer and instances of God at work.

Remember three golden rules. Keep worship:

- simple
- natural
- relevant

3. CONNECT YOUR COMMUNITY TO A LOCAL CHURCH

Let the community be a new congregation, group or worship service of a local church or congregation.

Forge mutually enriching relationships between the new community and the original congregation or church. For example:

- Social events can draw old and new Christians together.
- Small groups of new and long-standing believers can explore a shared interest, study the Bible, or organise an outreach activity (e.g. a bereavement support group).
- Some people may want to worship both in their new community and in another congregation or church that they are linked with.
- Leaders of new communities should meet with a church leader for mutual learning, encouragement and accountability.

Rather like the Trinity who are three persons united as one, a local church can be made up of multiple groups, communities, or congregations that are joined together.

4. REMEMBER THE MIXED ECONOMY OR BLENDED CHURCH!

New forms of church are not better than older ones. Nor are existing churches better than new ones.

In a blended, mixed economy, or mixed ecology church, each can enrich the other. New communities can reach people untouched by existing churches. Existing churches have centuries of wisdom that new communities can draw on.

Worried that a new Christian community will drain resources from the existing church? Instead, think of the opportunities.

True, Christians involved in new communities may have less time for activities within an established congregation.

However, by reaching new people, these communities will bring fresh gifts into the church. And this is the long-term answer to dwindling resources.

5. FOR EXAMPLE

A new Christian in Knit and Natter attends her new community on Tuesdays. She also goes to meetings of a conventional church on Mondays and Fridays. Perhaps one day she will be a key volunteer in the older church.

An Alpha congregation of people from outside the church started contributing to the finances of its parent congregation – music to a church treasurer's ears!

If your community does not have links with a specific local church, connect with other churches in the area, perhaps through local arrangements that bring churches together.

Or consider exploring links with one of the dispersed new (or traditional) monastic orders – e.g. Northumbria Community, Iona Community, Contemplative Fire, Franciscan Tertiaries.

6. ADVANTAGES

There are big advantages in starting a new Christian community rather than inviting people to an existing church:

- Individuals exploring Christianity can grow in faith where they are, rather than attend a church with unfamiliar people and practices
- What happens can be tailored to new believers' interests, questions, and where they are at
- They can more readily share their gifts and help lead the new community, strengthening their commitment and spiritual growth
- They can acquire habits of Christian behavior that fit their specific context. Rather than selling out to culture, new and existing Christians can discover how to live like Jesus within their culture
- Connections to the wider church will resource new believers' growth in Christian maturity
- If the new community comes to a natural end, these connections will offer pathways to another Christian gathering

7. AFRAID THESE NEW COMMUNITIES WILL DIVIDE THE CHURCH?

Remember: if a congregation insists that everyone worships together, it will face the even bigger danger of excluding lots of people. If you doubt this, re-read the Introduction.

Who decides when and where Christians worship, the type of music, length of talk and so on? Christians – us. Then we invite our friends. But the invitation is to come to church on our terms. Why should people come?

Even if they do, how can our church become their church? In practice, only if they fit in to what we have already decided. Is that what Christian inclusiveness is all about?

8. SO MAKE THE CHURCH INCLUSIVE

Prayerfully start a new Christian community at a time and place, with a style and agenda that work for people who find the existing church inaccessible. Jesus came for everybody. As his body, the church must be for everyone too.

DISCUSSION

Choose one or more of the following:

READ

Read Matthew 18.19-20. Spend time prayerfully reflecting on the phrase, 'For where two or three come together in my name, there am I with them.' Share any thoughts that come to you.

Imagine you invited some of your friends to the Sunday worship of a typical local church. (It might be yours!). What would they find surprising, helpful, and off-putting in the way that these Christians 'came together in Jesus' name'?

If these friends decided to follow Jesus, what would be a natural way for them to worship? For example:

- Might they prefer a sermon/talk, a podcast/video, a discussion, or some combination?
- Might they find it helpful to sing Christian songs/ hymns or listen to some Christian music? What type of Christian music might they prefer?
- Might they value combining worship with a meal or keeping the two separate?
- How might they pray – through spontaneous spoken prayers, written prayers, silent prayer, reflecting on a piece of Christian art, or some form of 'action prayer' (such as writing letters on behalf of Amnesty International, for example, and turning these letters into prayer)?
- What else would they find helpful?

In learning how to worship, what New Testament principles might they be advised to follow?

RESEARCH

Might you learn more about new Christian communities? For example, you or someone in the group could:

- Read one or more stories on the internet and report back to the group – e.g. Google 'fresh expressions stories'
- Select one of the Fresh Expressions videos for the group to watch:

  youtube.com/user/freshexpressions

- Invite someone leading a new Christian community to talk to your group
- Identify a new Christian community near you to visit

4. BASICS

RESOURCES FOR THE JOURNEY

Here's a way to journey with Jesus. Find a friend, love people round you, point them to Christ, and travel with them – at their pace – towards a new Christian community.

If you decide to come on this journey, you'll find it full of surprises. It may feel like you're making it up as you go along. God often surprises people.

But God is also at work in human plans. Jesus lived intentionally. He made plans to go to certain towns and villages, and sent his disciples ahead to prepare the ground. Towards the end of his life, Jesus planned to go to Jerusalem, even though he knew it wouldn't be easy.

If making plans was important for Jesus, should it not be important for us, too?

This chapter describes some kit to help you on your journey and plan your route.

- A compass to point you in the right direction
- A map to plan your course
- Food
- The address of your destination

Use these resources flexibly, especially the map. Use it to plot a path that works for you. But don't be surprised if the journey veers off unexpectedly.

One couple thought they were going to start a group with teenagers, but in the end a community of people with learning difficulties emerged.

So use the map, but allow the Spirit of God to take you on a detour!

ITEM 1. A COMPASS

This will steer you in the right direction. It comprises four values:

- Engage with people outside the church. Be missional.
- Love them in a way that fits their context and share Jesus in a manner they can understand. Be contextual.
- Encourage people to be open to Christ and allow him to form them in his likeness. Be formational.
- As people come to faith, help them – where they are – to become a Christian community connected to the wider church. You could become a new congregation, community or group within a local church, or sometimes a new church in your own right. Be ecclesial.

Sorted emerged among teenagers in Bradford, England. It was:

- Missional. The teenagers didn't go to church.
- Contextual. Activities, worship etc. were shaped by what the teenagers were in to.
- Formational. Teenagers were formed in the Christian faith.

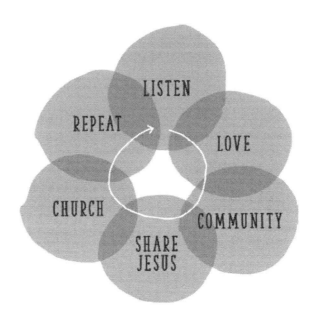

- Ecclesial. They didn't start going to an existing church. They became a new Christian community, with links to the wider church.

These four values will keep you heading in the right direction.

ITEM 2. A MAP

This loving-first cycle is like a map. It helps you plan your journey, recognise how far you've travelled, and decide where to go next.

As with any map, you can choose a wide variety of routes, but they have these features in common:

- You listen lovingly to God and to people round you
- Through listening, you prayerfully discover a simple way to love these people
- You build community with them in the process
- As trust deepens, you find natural opportunities to share Jesus together
- A new Christian community with the character of church takes shape among those coming to faith, where they are
- New believers repeat the cycle in their own way

All this is underpinned by prayer and ongoing connection to the wider church.

Of course, life is more messy than a diagram! So the circles may overlap, pile on top of each other, or sometimes happen in a different order. Quite often, teams re-focus on an earlier circle.

Each circle continues as the next is added – hence the overlaps.

The journey through these circles helps people experience a fuller life. As part of that, those who want to can get to know Jesus.

Don't feel you have to get to the end of the cycle! The main thing is that listen and love come first and motivate everything else.

Example – this is from Joe Pinnear in Luton, England:

- He listened to men who were into football. He hung out with them on Sunday nights, when they were at a loose end
- He loved them by bringing everyone together
- This deepened their sense of community
- They share Jesus as they sit round in their football gear before the match. They talk about Scripture and God's role in their lives
- This is laying the foundation for church – for a new worshipping community, connected to the Christian family

Thirst was a new Christian community among parents taking children to school. They met during the day when their children and partners couldn't come, so they repeated the cycle. They started an all-age community on Saturday afternoons, open to everyone.

The loving-first cycle is a vital piece of kit for starting a new Christian community. It is so important, in fact, that we have based Godsend on it. Each chapter contains stories and advice that will help you at the stage of the cycle you've reached.

ITEM 3. FOOD

Without nourishment, you'll fall by the wayside. Discovery Bible Study can be food for both you and those who join you.

A group of Christians advertised free canoeing on Sunday mornings. They paid for the canoe hire, and families enjoyed canoeing together. Sometimes over a picnic, the sessions finished with an all-age activity based on a Bible story or theme.

Tim then invited anyone interested to 'Food and Bible story' on Tuesday evenings. 'Bible story' included asking these four questions:

- If this story happened today, what would it look like?
- What is the story showing or telling me?
- Could it make a difference to my life? If so, how?
- Did it make a difference? If so, how?

Try using these questions in your core team as you discuss stories about Jesus and ones he told. Immerse yourselves in each story over several sessions.

Trying these questions, perhaps one per meeting, will give you the experience to help people who are new to the bible. Discovery Bible Study is your packed lunch to be shared with others.

(For other approaches, see Chapter 12.)

ITEM 4. THE ADDRESS OF YOUR DESTINATION

You need to know where you are going! The address is:

NEW CHRISTIAN COMMUNITY
GROWING IN FOUR SETS OF RELATIONSHIPS
WHICH LIE AT THE HEART OF CHURCH

These overlapping relationships are:

- With God directly in prayer, worship, and study
- With the outside world
- With the wider church
- Within the new community itself

Deepening these relationships will make your community an authentic part of the Christian family.

You'll be part of a mixed economy, mixed ecology or blended church. New and existing forms of church will exist alongside each other in relationships of mutual respect and support.

Anyone can do this!

You don't need:

- A degree in theology
- Special training
- An evangelism course
- Lots of Christian experience. In fact, you can do this if you have just become a Christian – or even if you are not yet a Christian and want to give Jesus a try!

But you do need the Spirit's help! So keep praying!

Remember: not everyone is called to this. And if you are, it may be for only a season.

Once called, here's your kit for the journey:

- The compass shows you the direction
- The map helps you plan your route
- Food nourishes you and those who join you
- The address helps you to know when you have reached your destination

Don't use the kit slavishly. Improvise, and you'll follow Jesus in a 21st century way.

DISCUSSION

Choose one or more of the following:

READ

Read Matthew 28.16-20. The Great Commission. Re-read it, keeping in mind the 'Basics' you have just explored. Then, using the 'Discovery Bible study' questions, discuss:

- If this story happened today, what would it look like?
- What is the story showing or telling us?
- Could it make a difference to our lives? How?

Before you next meet, spend time pondering the story and the discussion. Then, when you meet again:

- Either ask, 'Did the story make a difference? How?'
- Or ask: 'What thoughts has God prompted since we last met?'

IDEAS

Look at Chapter 10: Core Team. Being a strong team, even if it's only two of you, is really important. You may pick up some helpful ideas.

IMAGINE

Describe an aspect of your life that involves people who don't go to church – your work, family, friends you hang out with, your neighborhood, or an activity or interest you feel passionate about.

Imagine that God came to you in a dream and said that you could be part of a new Christian community in that context, and that the community could take any form you wanted.

- What would that community look like?
- How would it love other people in that context?
- What would people find attractive in that community?
- What next step might you take to turn that dream into reality?

5. REASONS

WHY IT MAKES SENSE

We have been thinking about a 21st century way to follow Jesus.

- Find one or more friends, and prayerfully listen to God and the context.

- Together, love the people round you.

- Make friends and build community with them.

- Over time, share stories about your faith.

- When people are ready, form a new Christian community where you are.

- And then, as suggested in the last chapter, encourage the new believers to repeat what you've done, but in their own way.

Actually, this is not just a 21st century way to follow Jesus, it's a first century recipe!

When Jesus sent his disciples to the towns and villages, they went in pairs (Luke 10.1-12). He didn't send them on their own. He told them to accept hospitality and heal the sick – to love people. As they did so, they would have made friends with them. They then announced the kingdom – they shared their faith in Jesus.

Note the order. Healing comes before announcing the kingdom (verse 9). They are following the loving-first cycle described in the last chapter!

After the disciples left each place, some people would have kept meeting together to prepare for Jesus' arrival. That's why the disciples went out in the first place (verse 1).

Later, when Jesus came he would had a huge impact on people, as he usually did (Luke 4.37). It's likely that those who had responded positively to him continued to meet where they lived. They would have discussed Jesus' teaching and encouraged each other to keep following him – just like new Christian communities today!

Following Jesus by travelling round the loving-first cycle is what the disciples did in Luke 12. Their first century way was appropriate to their context, and the twenty-first century approach described in Godsend fits ours today.

1. A STORY

Hot Chocolate in Dundee, Scotland, happened because intuitively a group of Christians travelled this loving-first missional journey:

- Some Christians listened to teenagers in the town center by taking them cups of hot chocolate. They discovered that the young people wanted a place to meet.
- They loved them by offering space in the church for them to hang out.

- They built community as they gathered.
- They shared Jesus by inviting those who wanted to know more to join the team in eating together, planning and worship.
- 'Church' emerged as the team became an expanding Christian community connected to the wider church.
- They have yet to repeat the cycle themselves, but they have been an inspiration to others.

2. IN ANY CONTEXT

This cycle is not just for young, white or suburban people, or for large churches or Christian enthusiasts. The Holy Spirit can enable you to use it in any setting.

- Focused on work? New Christian communities exist among offices workers, patients of a medical practice, and in schools.
- Concerned about homeless people? Abused women? Asylum seekers? LGBT+ community? Teenagers on an estate? People with learning difficulties? A small team can listen to them, love them, build community with them, introduce those interested to Jesus, and encourage a supportive Christian community to emerge.

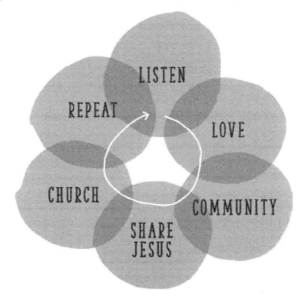

- Passionate about the environment, social justice or global poverty? Listen to people outside the church who share your heart, find ways to work together, form community as you do so, and explore how Christian spirituality can make a contribution.
- Into sport? Dog walking? Singing? Repairing bikes? People are starting new Christian communities in these and other activities.
- Live in a village? On an estate with multiple deprivation? Or belong to an ethnic minority? New Christian gatherings are emerging in these settings too.

New Christian communities are great because they take Jesus anywhere – to anyone.

3. THIS IS FULL-BLOODED KINGDOM DISCIPLESHIP

Each circle displays an aspect of God's kingdom.

- Listening shows love, a kingdom value
- Love includes pastoral care, environmental concern, and promoting social justice – all kingdom features
- Community is integral to the kingdom
- Sharing Jesus is sharing the person who announced that God's kingdom is near (Mark 1.15)
- Church happens when a new Christian community emerges and connects to the wider church. Kingdom and church will become one when Jesus returns
- Repeat witnesses to the expansive nature of the kingdom, which grows from a tiny seed into a huge tree (Matthew 13.31–32).

So each circle is not a mere stepping stone to the next, but has intrinsic kingdom value itself. Which means that each circle continues as others are added in (hence the overlap in the diagram).

What's more, Christian love and introducing people to Jesus are not kept separate, as often happens. They unite in a single process.

Some people think new Christian communities are too small to matter, but it's because they are often small that they do matter.

God seems to be using them to mobilize 'ordinary' Christians, in their daily lives, to be an answer to the prayer, 'Thy kingdom come.'

If you are committed to a larger congregation or church plant, don't think in either/or terms. Become a blended, mixed ecology or mixed economy church.

Combine your Sunday worship with kingdom discipleship in new, smaller communities in everyday life.

New Christian communities enable you to live out the kingdom more fully.

4. GENEROUS DISCIPLESHIP

The loving-first cycle is propelled by mutual generosity.

- Listening with no strings attached is an expression of generosity. It elicits generous responses of information, ideas, and a willingness to help. These form the basis of love.
- The generosity of love sparks further generosity – gifts of engagement, relationships and trust. These form the basis of community.
- The gift without strings of building community elicits responses that enrich the community – gifts of enjoyment, gratitude, increased trust and deepening relationships. These create an openness that makes sharing Jesus possible.
- The generous gift of sharing Jesus elicits the gifts of being enthused by Jesus and seeing him in ways that delight those who shared the gospel. These lay the foundation for 'church'.
- The generous offer of church, in the form of a new Christian community connected to the wider church, evokes responses of enthusiasm and joy.
- These encourage the journey to be repeated in a manner appropriate to the new context.

Each act of generosity ignites further generosity, and these become the basis of the next expression of generosity.

So the cycle echoes grace. God's generosity brings forth generous responses.

5. GOD SHOWERS THE WORLD WITH GIFTS

The church is one of these gifts – to Christians, but also to the world.

The church can be a gift by extending pastoral care, sharing its resources, and joining campaigns for social and ecological justice, for example. Many other organisations do much the same.

But there is one gift that only the church can offer – communal life with Jesus. No one else can offer being a sister or brother to Christ.

It's the most precious thing Christians can give. Because being family with Jesus is their very identity.

Offering something that valuable tells the other person how much they mean to you. You make a statement about how much the church treasures the world.

So follow the cycle and join in God's loving generosity!

6. DOING THIS ECHOES HOLY COMMUNION

Through the Spirit, you and your friend(s) are broken off from the congregation and offered as the body of Christ to people outside the church.

People gather round, receive the gift, 'consume' it in their own way and are transformed into a new Christian community.

Discipleship acquires a Holy Communion shape.

Some people worry that these new communities will celebrate Holy Communion infrequently, if at all. They won't be 'proper church'. But:

- New Christians can be introduced to sacramental worship in manageable steps. See Chapter 15.
- They can celebrate Communion with (or in) another congregation.
- 'Eucharistic grace' can extend from the wider church to the new community through the community's leaders, who may worship periodically in another congregation.
- Not least, as we have seen, starting a Christian community gives daily discipleship a Holy Communion tinge.

7. FOLLOWING JESUS

Following Jesus like this:

- Deepens discipleship
- Increases mission
- Grows the church, and above all
- Enriches people outside the church

DISCUSSION

Choose one or more of the following:

READ

Prayerfully read Mark 8.22-26. The healing of the blind man. Spend time quietly thinking about the story. The blind man's eyes were opened to see things he hadn't seen before.

- Have your eyes been opened by the Godsend material you have been seeing and reading? In what ways?
- Are there things you are beginning to see, but not very clearly?
- Jesus had to repeat the healing process before the man could see. Which parts of Godsend might you have to go over again before you see more clearly?

IMAGINE

Prayerfully imagine a scale of 1–10, where 1 = opposed to new Christian communities, 5 = open to them, and 10 = very enthusiastic about them.

- Before you started this chapter, where were you on that scale?
- Where would you put yourself now?
- What has influenced you to change or stay the same?
- What doubts and questions remain?
- Where might you get answers to these doubts/ questions? For example...

Explore other parts of the app? Which topics?
Visit a new Christian community?
Read or watch online some stories about them?
Speak to someone with more experience of these communities? Who?

LISTEN

6. CALLED?

COUNTING THE COST

Do you sometimes think you were put on this planet for a deeper purpose? Do you wish you could impact the world for good?

Maybe you've heard about new Christian communities among parents in schools, artists, in food banks or in other walks of life.

These communities are an opportunity to represent Jesus to people, and to be a godsend to all involved.

Could God want you to be involved?

These communities are great, but they're also a challenge:

- Sometimes they're tough going
- They immerse you deeply in people's lives
- You may have to reorganise your life around theirs

If you weren't called to this, why would you do it?

But if you are called, and God is behind it, don't miss this opportunity – it could change the world...

NEW CHRISTIAN COMMUNITIES HAVE MANY NAMES

They can be called fresh expressions of church, missional communities, church plants, new worshipping congregations, emerging churches and more.

They arise prayerfully among people who don't do church. Often the communities are linked to an existing local church, but take a different form.

Typically, two or more Christians:

- Listen – they ask God to reveal a need or hope in their context
- Find a simple way to respond in love
- Create community with people in the process
- Invite those involved to talk about life and faith – as this happens, they share Jesus
- Encourage a Christian community, connected to the wider church, to form round those coming to Jesus – this may be a group or congregation of a local church, or a new church in its own right
- Inspire the community to repeat the process in its own way

All this is underpinned by prayer and connection to the wider Christian family.

These communities emerge around what the Spirit is already doing in the world. So being 'called' is God's invitation to join in with the Spirit.

There are two aspects: first, are you yourself called to help start a new Christian community?

Secondly, as you and the core team discuss possibilities with others in the context, how is the Spirit calling you to birth this community?

In practice, the two are often tangled together.

DISCOVERING GOD'S CALL IS A VOYAGE

You journey from your existing church involvement to a new one – helping to start a new Christian community.

What's involved?

Dissatisfaction with the status quo propels the voyage. You feel that there is more for you and other people round you.

> **Caution!** Some new communities flounder because the Christian core is united by dissatisfaction with the existing church, but not much else. Holy discontent is not negativism. It fuels a passion for change.

Exploration is central to the voyage.You imagine different destinations – different ways of serving God and different forms a new Christian community might take. Prayerfully you explore the possibilities. 'What's God asking me/us to do?'

Sense-making stories are one of the results of the voyage. You and your core team tell stories about what you hope for and why, and you tell them to different audiences:

- To yourselves
- To the people you feel called to
- To your family and friends
- To your church leaders (if you are part of a local church)
- To others involved

The stories may differ, but this doesn't matter provided they are consistent and make sense to their audiences.

Often at first these stories are about loving people and getting to know them better; only later do they include chapters about exploring Jesus and becoming a Christian community.

You don't have to imagine the ending before you start. Indeed, like any good story, the ending may be a surprise!

RESPONDING TO GOD'S CALL ISN'T ALWAYS EASY

You may have to re-focus your priorities. You may have less time for other commitments (including your local church, perhaps). Reshaping your priorities is vital – but can be hard.

You may have to give up some of your ideas. As you listen to people round you, you may come to think differently about the best way to love them.You thought you were called to start a Messy Church, for example, but comments from families suggest something else.

You may have to give up some of your preferences. You may have to rethink what being a Christian community or 'church' will look like for the people you are called to. Perhaps it's not what you're used to. Just as Jesus died so that we might live, some of your preferences may have to die so that he can bring life to others.

Example – Paul Unsworth, a Baptist minister, loved preaching, but dropped this idea in Kahaila Cafe's Wednesday evening worship. People engaged more with the Christian faith through discussion.

You may well have to be patient. New Christian communities do not emerge overnight.

WHAT DOES GOD WANT YOU TO DO?

Prayerfully consider if any of these signs apply to you.

You feel dissatisfied.

- You suspect there's more to life
- You long for your faith to link better to everyday experience
- You wish you could do more to make the world a better place
- The church is not connecting with your friends
- You are looking for new opportunities to show God's love

Discontent can be God spurring you on!

You know someone else who feels the same.

Often it is hard to soldier on alone.But the unexpected becomes possible when two or three people band together. That's why Jesus sent his apprentices out in pairs (Luke 10.1).

You have a passion for a group of people whose lives you'd love to enrich. Most new Christian communities are started among people the founders already know.

What possibilities come to mind? (The more specific the group the better.)

- People you rarely notice?
- Your neighbourhood?
- Friends?
- Others who share your passion?
- People you volunteer with?
- People who break your heart?
- Your workplace?

Check Chapter 8: Ideas (on page 64).

Others confirm you are onto something.

You feel energised by the possibility.

The idea will not leave your head.

Don't be discouraged if all these (and other) signs are not present now. God's call feels different for different people and grows over time.

WHO MIGHT HELP YOU NAVIGATE THE VOYAGE?

Could you chat to a trusted Christian from time to time?

Might you study other topics in Godsend to understand better what's involved?

Can you speak to someone who has started a new Christian community?

Could you speak to your church leader?

KEEP PRAYING!

Go to 24-7prayer.com for ideas on how to pray.

New Christian communities come from God, so lay deep foundations of prayer.

DISCUSSION

Choose one or more of the following:

READ

Prayerfully read Acts 13.1-3, where Barnabas and Paul are sent off, and then ask:

- If this story happened in your church today, what would it look like?
- In re-telling this story, what is important?
- How do you as an individual or group discern what the Spirit is calling you to?
- Who might you ask to support you in prayer as you discern God's will in relation to starting a new Christian community?

PRAY

Whether you've tried this before or not, prayer is about figuring out what you really long for – for other people, the world and yourself. Then you speak it, write it, draw it, imagine it or express it in some way to God. You can pray on your own, and you can pray with others.

Focus on what God is calling you to. Stay silent with each other. Close your eyes for 5 minutes – set your phone to beep! Then share what longings came to mind. Draw them, speak them out, or write them down – whatever feels comfortable.

If you are using Godsend with one or more others, why not pray on your own like this every day till you next meet? Keep a note of what emerges and share it with one another.

- Are any patterns emerging from your praying?
- What do you long for most deeply for other people round you?
- What do you long for most deeply for yourself?
- What action do you think God's voice of love may be calling you to take?

Individually or as a group, you may find taketime.org.uk helpful in meditating and listening to God.

TEST YOUR CALL

If you feel yourself being called to help start a new Christian community:

- Ask yourself: Who can I discuss this with?
- Check the resources on fxresourcing.org to help you prayerfully think further
- Read one or more of the following:

Michael Beck and Michael Moynagh, *The 21st Century Christian: Following Jesus Where Life Happens* (Fresh Expressions US, 2020) – all you need to know about the why and how of new Christian communities.

Barbara Glasson, *Mixed-up Blessing: A New Encounter with Being Church* (Inspire, 2006) – an inspirational story of bread church, a classic.

Andy Milne, *The DNA of Pioneer Ministry* (SCM Press, 2016) – tells the story of Sorted, a new community among teenagers, drawing out key principles.

Michael Moynagh, *Church in Life: Innovation, Mission and Ecclesiology* (SCM Press, 2017) – more academic, but packed full of theology and principles for action, with case studies.

7. STARTING

AN ABC GUIDE

New Christian communities connect faith to life. They make a difference and introduce people to Jesus.

Do you think this is too difficult for you?

It can be dead easy!

Why not team up with someone and give away cakes in your street or at work? Do you have a neighbour who needs cheering up, or does somebody have a birthday coming up?

Do you enjoy listening to music? Why not host a house gig with bring-and-share food, and afterwards talk about the music together?

With a little planning, it's possible to get people together around something they enjoy or care about. What are people round you into? Spread the word locally and see who gets in touch.

Keep it simple. Start prayerfully with what you've got – who you are, what you know and who you know. Then listen carefully to what people think of your ideas.

You can do it!

It's a simple as A,B,C.

A.SK GOD AND ASK A FRIEND

New Christian communities are a work of God. So to start one you need God's guidance.

Prayer is vital.

Keep asking God, 'Who are you bringing to my attention?' 'What do you want me to do next?'

God wants us to work in teams.

In the beginning God said to Adam, 'It is not good for the man to be alone' (Genesis 2.18).

God's huge project – to fill the world with human beings and spread the Garden of Eden over the whole globe – was launched with just two people.

You don't need a large team to start a new Christian community. Equally, you can't do it on your own.

You'll need support.

Behind the team you also need people who will pray for you. This is often forgotten, but it is absolutely vital! So ask some friends to pray regularly for you, and keep them in touch with what you are doing.

Caution! If you have a large team, think about the pitfalls:

- People may have different agendas.
- Their networks may not gel together.
- Pastorally supporting the team may divert leaders from those beyond the team you want to connect with.
- The team may become preoccupied with its own needs.
- The team's worship may not suit newcomers or easily adapt to them.

On the other hand, a large team could break into smaller hubs, each with its own missional focus. Hubs might meet together once or twice a month for support, learning, and vision sharing. The team would birth several new communities!

B.EGIN WITH WHAT YOU'VE GOT

Don't stare at a blank piece of paper. Start with what God has given you. What have you got in your hands, and whose hands do you shake? So prayerfully ask:

Who are we?

- What are the opportunities where we live or work?
- What are our passions? Cooking? Photography? Football? Could we share these with our work colleagues, for example?

What do we know about?

- Music? Building websites? Who could we share these skills with?
- What do we know about other new Christian communities? Could we adapt what's worked elsewhere?

Who do we know?

- Who could we share our passion or knowledge with?
- Who could we ask to help? For example, say you go cycling with friends. Might some people organize food for everyone when the cyclists return? As you eat together, you would deepen community.

What do we have?

- A home to meet in?
- A car to transport people?
- Time to spend with others?

> **Example –** Take Louisa. **Who was she?** A community nurse in a medical practice. **What did she know?** That an unusually high number of new mothers suffered from depression. **Who did she know?** Charlie and Charlotte. They lived near the mums. The three of them came up with the idea of starting a support group for new mothers. **What did they have?** Charlie and Charlotte's home. So they started a support group in Charlie and Charlotte's home. And in time it evolved into a Christian community.

Let God speak to you through what you've got. Remember: you don't have to do all the giving. Let others help you.

> **Caution!** Ask whether your demographic focus is sufficiently narrow to guide what you do. Or does it contain lots of sub-groups of people, each of whom can be reached in a different way? If so, would it help to narrow your focus further?

C.HAT AND LISTEN TO OTHERS

This is our middle heading because it is the heart of everything.

Keep listening and talking in four directions:

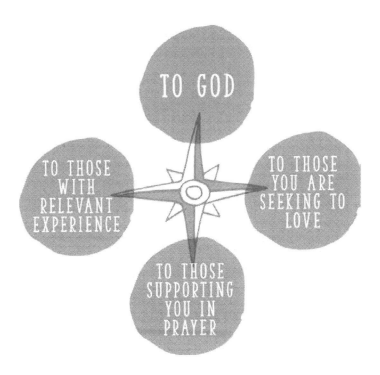

- To God directly in prayer
- To those you are seeking to love. Don't assume you know what to do. Let them tell you. Every time you get stuck, ask them for the solution
- To those supporting you in prayer. Don't forget the importance of prayer support!
- To those with relevant experience in the wider church and elsewhere. Their wisdom may be invaluable

Caution! Don't be too quick to copy others. What worked for them may not be the best way to love people where you are. Ask the people you're called to what they think.

A Cambridge psychologist, Dr Sarah Savage, said: 'The experience of being listened to well is as close to the experience of being loved as to be barely indistinguishable.'

So listen carefully.

Example: Hot Chocolate started with some Christians offering cups of hot chocolate to young people in Dundee city centre. The Christians discovered that the young people were looking for a place to rehearse their band, and offered them the church building. This was the beginning of what became a thriving community, with a worshipping core. It started with what the Christians knew – how to make hot chocolate! But it developed because they listened to the young people and responded to them.

DREAM UP LOTS OF IDEAS

Ask 'What if...?' 'What if we did this?' 'What if we did that?' Stretch your imagination.

'Expert designers keep asking, "What if?" Inexperienced ones stop too soon and miss out on creative possibilities (Nigel Cross, *Design Thinking*, Bloomsbury, 2011).

You are designing a new Christian community. So keep brainstorming 'What if?' until you go 'Wow!'

Then see if it works.

What if? What wows? What works?

EXPERIMENT LIKE CRAZY

This is the fastest way to learn.

New Christian communities emerge through trial and error. Remember: it's trial *and error!*

You can be disappointed in the results of an experiment. But it's not failure if you learn from them.

So don't use the word 'failure'. Talk about disappointment.

And remember: there is no such thing as failure, only feedback.

F.OLLOW THE LOVING-FIRST CYCLE

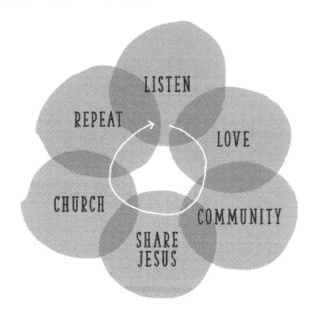

G.OD IS THE BOTTOM LINE

So make prayer a priority.

Do you have a group of people who are praying for your initiative?

DISCUSSION

Choose one or more of the following:

READ

Read Luke 2.41-52 prayerfully. Jesus provides an example of listening to culture.

- If this story happened today, what would it look like?
- In retelling this story, what strikes you as important in the way that Jesus listened?
- If you are starting a new Christian community, how might this story influence the way you listen to people?

REFLECT

- Is listening just about what you hear? What about what you feel or see?
- How attentively do you listen to all the voices of people working with you?
- Who has been a good listener to you and what can you learn from that person?

THINK

Prayerfully think of different aspects of your life – work, where you live, your leisure pursuits, friendship networks, things you are passionate about...

- Whom might you team up with in one of these parts of your life?
- Work your way through the Guide with that person.

JOURNAL

Start a journal, noting down who and what you are being drawn to.

- Use the headings in the Guide to structure your jottings.
- Prayerfully look for any patterns.
- Do these patterns suggest how God might be leading you?

PICTURE IT!

Picture the context you feel called to serve.

- What are the three best things about it?
- What could you do to make it better?
- If you did this, what would be your dream outcome?
- Who could help you to achieve that dream? Someone who has helped you before?

LOVE

8. IDEAS

STORIES TO INSPIRE YOU

Beware of rushing in to build community and share faith with people. These are great things to do. But you can only build community and share your faith if you have loved people first.

When Jesus taught his disciples to do mission in Luke 10, he told them to first heal the sick and then announce the kingdom.

He himself loved people unconditionally and healed them unconditionally. All the 10 lepers were healed, even though only one came back to thank Jesus.

Love is the most important thing.

The church has become so distant from most people that it's lost its credibility. People don't know the church, so why would they trust it? To bridge the gap, you have to start with love.

To make a difference to people, we need to have meaningful relationships with them. So build these through practical love.

Love can unlock people's hearts, so that they are open to stories about Jesus.

So look for simple ways to serve people, and let community form as people gather round your activity of love.

Love was the top priority for Jesus. Make it your top priority too.

Start by thinking of an idea.

1. STRUGGLING TO COME UP WITH AN IDEA?

Maybe your imagination is limited by your experience.

If so, don't be constrained by the walled garden of what you know. Break out and explore the possibilities beyond.

Look at:

- The dreams and longings of the people around you
- What works well outside the church
- What other Christians have done

And don't just imitate one idea. Mix the ideas up and open the door to a whole new world.

2. A PLACE TO MEET

Often people long to hang out – to meet other families, get to know their neighbours, make friends or chat longer with workmates.

Why not respond to that need?

For example, a young adult made soup and invited the neighbours to connect.

A couple hosted a monthly community breakfast in their home for people in nearby streets.

Parents formed Thirst by meeting weekly in the school staff room for coffee, croissants, laughter, and chat.

A couple offered lemonade and cookies at the front of their home for latchkey kids after school.

Why not download Meetup or a similar app to hook up with people near you? – visit meetup.com/apps

Many new Christian communities are 'third spaces'. The first space is home, the second is work and the third is a space where you relax with others.

3. TAKE YOUR PASSION A STEP FURTHER

You could form a group round your interest or hobby, such as Knit and Natter, which started with people from outside church gathering to knit. A simple devotion at the end proved popular. Step by step it evolved into a new Christian community.

New Christian communities have begun to emerge among walkers, card makers, felt makers and people using a gym.

If you go walking with friends, take a picnic or go out for a meal when you return. Eat together and get to know each other.

If you coach a sports team, you could team up with friends to provide food when the session is over.

Do you enjoy repairing bikes? Why not teach local teenagers to repair theirs and chat with them while doing so?

4. PEOPLE ON THE EDGE OF SOCIETY

Saturday Gathering started among clients of a Saturday morning food bank. People eat together in the same venue on Saturday evenings, share their experiences and explore the Bible.

In West London, homeless people and others gather for Sunday afternoon tea and then sit round tables for worship.

Do you have a passion for vulnerable people, asylum seekers, unemployed young adults, or residents on a tough housing estate? Ask how you can support or add to existing initiatives among them.

Or might you share a skill or interest – perhaps teach photography to unemployed teenagers? Or run a language cafe? Recent migrants could practice their English over afternoon tea.

5. SOCIAL AND ENVIRONMENTAL JUSTICE

Are you passionate about global poverty, modern slavery or climate change? If so, why not use social media to find others who are too? Arrange a get together to share ideas, plan some action, and explore spirituality to resource the group.

Just Church began with people writing letters on behalf of Amnesty International. These letters were their enacted prayers.

One person gathered a group of men to clean up and improve the neighbourhood. They met in the pub afterwards and discussed how to improve as fathers, partners, and at work.

6. SOMETHING AT WORK

Communities are emerging among patients of a medical practice (Google 'Coffee in the Living Room Christ Church Bayston Hill'), children at school, and as 'spirituality at work'.

Gather people into:

- A Christian meditation group during the lunch hour
- A community choir
- A film club (watch a film one week, discuss it over a drink the next)
- A CPD group to discuss articles relevant to your professional development (and count it toward your points!)

If you own a business, might you offer a voluntary course on Christian mindfulness to your staff in company time?

7. SOMETHING SIMPLE

Give away free cakes in your neighbourhood, as mentioned in the last chapter. When asked why you do this, reply: 'If you want to know, come to our planning meetings. We eat cake, drink wine, have fun and explore spirituality.'

Anyone can do this, whatever their tradition and however little they think they know about the Christian faith!

8. AN EXISTING INITIATIVE OR PROJECT

Maybe you're involved in a Christian outreach project.

No need to think up something new. You are already engaged in practical love.

Maybe the idea you now need is how to introduce an opportunity for people to explore Jesus.

For example

- A lunch club, bereavement group or drop-in centre might invite guests to a short spiritual reflection immediately beforehand or afterwards.
- A Christian leader of a uniformed organization might invite those who attend to a separate 'pizza and share' event (having thought about the safeguarding implications). Young people might share what was going on for each of them, and a different person might pray after each one had shared. (One youth worker did this with teenagers from outside the church, and they loved it!)
- A church-run coffee shop might invite customers to a weekly discussion evening on a news topic with a spiritual angle. To make it a conversation with a difference, halfway through ask, 'If God existed, what would he/she/it think about what we've been saying?'

Look at Chapters 7 and 8, and ask what ideas might be relevant to your initiative.

Caution. Remember: you can't impose your Christian agenda if the group is meeting for a different purpose. But you may be able to do something alongside the group. Only introduce something into the main meeting if you have the group's permission.

9. STILL CAN'T THINK OF SOMETHING?

Why not gather some people, have a drink and ask them, 'What needs improving round here?'

Don't come up with ideas for the people you know. Generate ideas with them!

DISCUSSION

Choose one or more of the following:

READ

Prayerfully read Matthew 25.31-46 (Jesus identifies himself with the weakest and most vulnerable).

- Who are the weakest among the people you are seeking to serve – whether at work, in your network, in your apartment block, or those who share your passion?
- For you, what would be the equivalent of feeding them, inviting them in, clothing them, looking after them, and coming to them in their own particular prisons?
- What weaknesses might you share with them so that they can help you?

IMAGINE

Imagine that while you are asleep a miracle happens and your wildest dream for your context is fulfilled.

- Who would be first to notice?
- What would they see, hear, and feel that would tell them that the miracle had happened?
- If 10 represents the day after the miracle and 1 is the furthest away from the miracle you could be, where would you rate things now?
- If you put the number one point higher up the scale, what would be happening differently?
- What's happening now that would help you move to that point?

STUCK FOR AN IDEA?

Don't be discouraged! Wait patiently for the Spirit, and use events in your everyday life to trigger ideas. For example:

- Imagine your team/core group envisages an initiative among teenagers. Later you are on a bus. 'What if we used a bus to reach young people?' you might think.
- Then you go out for a meal. 'What if we held curry evenings for teenagers?'
- You return home and find the family watching football. 'What if we start a soccer team?'
- The next day you enter the office. 'What if we developed work experience opportunities?'

EMERGING THEMES

Might your team/core group prayerfully do something like this?

- People could bring their favourite what ifs? to the next meeting and pool their ideas.
- As you sift ideas, make a list of why nots? and what's good? – 'why not this idea?' 'what's good about it?'
- Then ask what themes emerge from these lists. Do these themes begin to clarify what you are looking for?
- Try repeating the process over several meetings.

DISCUSSING IT

If you've got an idea, who else might you discuss it with:

- One of those you are called to serve?
- Others with experience of your context?
- Someone with experience of new Christian communities?
- Someone familiar with a similar demographic group?
- Those who are praying for you? (Have you set this up?)

- A trusted Christian friend or leader?
- Your mentor/coach? (Might you find a mentor/coach?)

REFLECTION

For reflection. When you begin to love others:

- Will you ask them for their feedback, so that you can improve what you do? How keen are you to learn from those you lovingly serve?
- Will you encourage people to volunteer to help? Or will you go further and invite some of them to help lead the initiative?
- How far will this be your project and how far will it be theirs? Where will power lie?

9. INNOVATE

HOW TO START SOMETHING NEW

So you're looking for ways to love people around you? How could the Holy Spirit help?

The Spirit is constantly inspiring people to innovate in the name of love. All with one goal, to bring about the kingdom of God.

This kingdom is like a great feast where the doors are thrown open to welcome everyone so the hungry are fed and nobody goes without.

It's like a tiny seed that looks unpromising at first but grows into a huge tree where birds and animals come and go. The kingdom grows from something small into something that changes the ecosystem of the whole planet.

This kingdom is new.

It's innovation on a cosmic scale!

The Spirit is bringing it to birth with innovation all over the place. Bit by bit the Spirit is reconfiguring what exists now till it reflects God's character of love.

That's what innovation is all about – putting things together in new and original ways. Innovation changes 'the rules of the game' for doing something – either radically or incrementally.

Your practical love could change the rules of the game for what happens round you – in a small way or more dramatically.

God is the ultimate Innovator and we are made in God's image to innovate too. As the Spirit reassembles creation in new ways, God invites us in the name of love to join in.

So if you are looking to love people round you pray, listen to the Spirit, take courage and innovate!

How might you start?

- Pray that God will stretch your imagination
- Don't just copy what others have done. Be ready for God to show you something fresh
- And learn how innovation works. It involves six overlapping processes

1. DISSATISFACTION

Holy or prophetic discontent is vital.

You would not start anything new unless you were dissatisfied with what exists. The status quo is not working properly, or it could be so much better.

That was Caroline's experience. She was a school teacher in

north-west London. Around her were a growing number of people from ethnic minority backgrounds.

She felt frustrated because her local church had so little contact with this changing population. Her discontent fuelled her determination to do something about it.

The old must be revealed as inadequate before the new is born.

2. EXPLORATION

Caroline began to explore how her church might make connections with its new neighbours.

She started with what she'd got:

- Who was she? A primary school teacher
- What did she know? That many of her children's mothers could not speak English well. She also knew how to teach. Could she use her teaching skills to help these women learn better English?
- Who did she know? People in the church who might be willing to help her

She kept thinking of different possibilities until she hit on the idea of a language cafe – invite the women to an English afternoon tea, sit them round tables, and encourage them to discuss a topic in English.

Caroline didn't waste time coming up with ideas beyond her resources. Nor did she try something outside her expertise. She built on what she knew.

Then she tried the idea on others, listened to their responses, and launched an experiment.

3. SENSE-MAKING

Caroline told stories to make sense of what she was doing.

Eventually, she told three stories:

- To her church: 'For over a hundred years we've supported overseas mission. Overseas is now on our doorstep. What are we going to do about it?'
- To the mothers: 'Welcome to this part of London. You are invited to an English afternoon tea, where you can learn English.'
- To herself: 'In Jesus, God went out to people. We're trying something similar.'

Think about this: People follow stories rather than leaders. So be intentional about your stories!

Listen carefully to the groups you're in touch with, discover what they are into and craft different, but consistent, stories that connect with their priorities.

4. AMPLIFICATION

When a story grabs people's imagination, it spreads and motivates people to get involved. It amplifies.

Perhaps one of Caroline's mothers said, "Have you heard there's a free afternoon tea on Thursday and they're going to help us learn English? Would you like to come?"

It was a good story and people came.

So develop a compelling story. Try it out on people. See how they react. And change it to meet their reservations. Keep doing this till your story gets an enthusiastic response.

Don't forget "people of peace" (Luke 10.6)! They know lots of people and will retell your story to them.

Find someone with plenty of contacts, tell a story that engages them, and your story will spread like wildfire.

5. EDGE OF CHAOS

Edge of chaos is the boundary between order and chaos. Too much order, and you get stuck in a rut. Too much change, and your community becomes chaotic; people can't cope.

Don't let your new Christian community become too orderly. If it does, it may become stale and miss out on new opportunities.

Caroline's could have settled into an unchanging weekly routine – welcome people, serve tea, encourage guests to discuss a topic in English, clear up afterwards.

But Caroline wanted more. She kept herself on the edge of chaos.

Through a surprise conversation, she and her team decided to set up a prayer board.

The women pinned prayer requests to the board and discussed them. This raised the cafe's spiritual temperature and helped pave the way for a separate Alpha course for the cafe's guests.

The cafe moved forward because Caroline refused to be stuck.

6. TRANSFORMATION

Innovation changes those involved.

- Some of Caroline's mothers attended the Alpha course and continued to meet for Bible study.
- Her volunteer helpers became more confident.
- So did Caroline. Before starting the cafe, she saw herself as someone in the pews with gifts. Afterwards, she saw herself as having the ability to lead something new.
- Her local church gained confidence in mission. This helped it to start a Messy Church and a debt counselling centre.

Innovation need not threaten tradition. It can enable a tradition to express itself in new ways.

7. THE INNOVATOR'S MINDSET

Dissatisfaction, exploration, sense-making, amplification, edge of chaos and transformation all overlap and apply to any type of innovation, large or small.

They comprise the innovator's mindset, which you may prayerfully need to love people round you. It is very different to the manager's mindset. The lists below show the contrasting elements which make up these mindsets:

INNOVATOR'S MINDSET

- Feels dissatisfied with the status quo

- Improvises

- Sees 'failure' as learning

- Creates new stories

- Seeks feedback from people round about

- Embraces edge of chaos

- Changes what exists

MANAGER'S MINDSET

- Facilitates the status quo

- Sets objectives

- Avoids mistakes

- Works within the organisation's story

- Seeks permission from people higher up

- Values certainty

- Guides what exists

The bottom line? You need both, depending on the circumstances.

DISCUSSION

Choose one or more of the following:

COSMIC SCALE

Think prayerfully about the statement in the animation, 'The kingdom of God is innovation on a cosmic scale.'

- What excites you about it?
- What challenges you?
- What reservations do you have?

How might your answers influence your search for a way to love people round you?

YOUR CONTEXT

Discuss makes you dissatisfied about your context.

EXPLORATION

Discuss what stands out for you about the process of exploration. What might your core team do differently as a result?

STORIES

Discuss your reactions to the statement, 'People follow stories rather than leaders' (taken from the book *Leading by Story* by Vaughan S Roberts and David Simms, SCM Press, 2017).

- What part does story-telling play in bringing about something new?

- What stories are you starting to tell about your initiative?
- What criteria would you use to decide whether they are good stories?
- How might you improve your stories?

INNOVATOR V MANAGER

In what situations are the innovators' and managers' mindsets most appropriate?

- To which mindset do you and others in your core team most naturally gravitate?
- What are your priority tasks in the coming months, and which of the two mindsets will you most need to fulfil them?
- How can you make sure the two mindsets work together in doing these tasks?

COMMUNITY

10. CORE TEAM

TURNING TEAM INTO COMMUNITY

Do you want to change the world? Community is key.

A while back some Christians in a large company got together to support their colleagues who'd been made redundant. They paid for each person to have free advice.

Others commented, 'These Christians are better than our HR department!'

One person alone couldn't have provided this support. A group was necessary. Practical love often requires community.

This is true even of God. Look at Jesus. He was constantly communicating with his Father and being led by the Spirit, and it was as part of this divine community that he poured out his love.

Brazilian theologian, Leonardo Boff, said: 'Father, Son and Holy Spirit are always together: they create together, save together, and together bring us into their communion of life and love.'

Just note how close they are. Father, Son and Spirit act as one. God is three persons in total union.

It is not just community that changes the world. It is intimate community. If you want to change the world, take a leaf from God's book – and begin with your team. The next chapter, Chapter 11: Community (page 89), is about building community among the people the core team serves.

1. COMMUNITY STARTS WITH THE TEAM

Through listening and love, you will start to form community with the people you are called to.

Deep community begins with your team/core group because it is the hub of the community and sets the tone.

The quality of your team's communal life will ripple out to others, just as the communal life of the Trinity overflows into the world.

2. MAKE 'COMMUNITY' RATHER THAN 'TEAM' A PRIORITY

Teams become communities when their members relate primarily not to their leaders but to one another.

In a team, the leader is the focal person. The leader makes the decisions (hopefully after consulting the team).

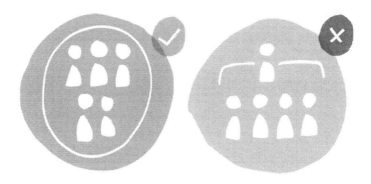

In a community, leaders have an important role but they are not the focal point. Members relate mainly to each other. Decision-making is shared.

One study found that in effective teams, people held little side conversations while others were contributing to the discussion (Alex Pentland, *Social Physics: How Social Networks Can Make Us Smarter*, New York: Penguin Press, 2014, pp. 88–89). There was a community feel.

You can encourage community by inviting people to check in whenever the core team meets. To help people understand each other more in the round, ask members to share:

- The most challenging thing and the best thing that has happened since they last met, or
- Where they have seen God at work since they last met

Teams also become communities when fellow members matter at least as much as the task. Members do favours and look out for each other.

They go the second mile for one another. They commit themselves to team relationships, not just to the team's goals.

Caution! Beware of running away from conflict. To protect their relationships, people may avoid conflict or criticising one another's performances. This hinders learning. So don't forget the task! Communities can be energised by a shared goal.

3. EXPERIENCES BEFORE VALUES IS A GOOD MOTTO

Many teams assume their first job is to become clear about their purpose and values. But done too early, this may produce needless and fruitless debate.

Different personalities, experiences and expectations may block agreement. Or some members may go along with the others but without being deeply committed to the decision. When things get tough, they disengage or drop out.

So instead, start by banking some shared experiences:

- eating together
- a film night
- going on a day trip
- learning about one another's past experiences, especially of teams

To avoid frustration that you are neglecting the task, the team can explore its purpose but as a secondary activity.

Shared experiences help to create good relationships so that you can discuss objectives and values honestly.

4. LEARN TOGETHER PRAYERFULLY

Some people assume the team's main task is its goals, but achievement is only possible if the team learns as it goes along.

So make learning your priority.

Look at all the learning that happened when the first churches were planted! Not for nothing did the Christians call themselves 'disciples', which comes from the Latin word for 'learning'.

Your core team can encourage learning by regularly holding 'milestone reviews', in which members ask three questions:

- **What is?** What happened since we last met? Did we achieve what we hoped? What can we learn?

- **What could be?** What are the possibilities and options going forward?
- **What will be?** What actions shall we commit ourselves to?

Milestone reviews can be undertaken informally by two friends over a coffee, or formally as an agenda item in a meeting.

5. WELCOME DISAGREEMENT AS:

- An opportunity to learn from other points of view.
- A sign that individuals are being given space – their views are not ignored or suppressed.
- A mark of honest sharing, which deepens relationships as different opinions are expressed.
- A school in managing conflict – members can apply what they've learnt in the core team to their other relationships. For example, lessons about handling disagreement well can be taken into the community that forms round the team's practical love.

When a discussion gets painfully tense, have a period of prayerful silence.

This can still emotions, allow members to address their inner hearts, encourage everyone to become more open to other views, and give space to hear the Spirit.

6. MIGHT ONE OF THE TEAM BE "CHAPLAIN"...

... to nurture the community's spiritual life?

It doesn't have to be the leader!

Remember: fruitful Christian communities all seem to have prayer at their heart.

DISCUSSION

Choose one or more of the following:

READ

Prayerfully read Matthew 18.21-35 (the unmerciful servant).

- Imagine an equivalent story in the context of your core group/team's life. What would it look like?
- List what is involved in the process of forgiveness.
- How might you encourage each other to practice this 'holy habit' of forgiveness?

REFLECT

- What other holy habits might you encourage in your core group/team?
- Might you ask someone in the team to be especially responsible for encouraging holy habits within the team?
- Might you ask someone from outside to be a mentor to your team/core group?
- How might tools like the taketime website help you in meditating/listening to God?

SHARE

Invite others in the team/core group to prayerfully share their best experience of being in a team or group.

- Having listened to each other's stories, what lessons might you learn?
- How might you incorporate these lessons into your team's life?

RESEARCH

Ask a team member to research:

- Someone good at nurturing team life who could be invited to share their experience, or
- A helpful YouTube video to watch, or
- A blog or book chapter to discuss

11.
COMMUNITY
"HOME" FOR THOSE INVOLVED

Each day we meet lots of people – shop assistants, bus drivers, school teachers, work colleagues, and many more.

We don't really know most of them, just what they do. We put them into a box without thinking about their families, their interests and all the other things that make up their unique identities.

That's inevitable, of course. If you get on the bus and ask the driver how her family is, what she wants to do with her life... The queue would be huge!

Perhaps it's a good thing that we don't always know everything about each other. But sometimes it can feel as if we're only known for what we do rather than who we are.

In fact, most people don't know us very well at all.

Jesus gathered a community round him, and grew deep relationships with his followers through which they really got to know one another. And he taught them to grow deep relationships with other people too.

Jesus' heart is for us to form communities, in which each person is known and loved just as they are.

So make this a priority for you, too.

1. THE SECRET OF COMMUNITY

Hospitality is the key to community. It goes beyond welcoming new arrivals. It's a deeply ingrained, constant attitude of welcome toward the other person.

In a healthy community, both newcomers and long-standing members are always made to feel at home. They are well known and deeply loved, warts and all.

Feeling at home is more likely the longer people spend with each other. So how might members of your community spend more time together?

Some examples

- More use of social media?
- Eating together regularly?
- Film evenings and the like?
- Day trips?
- A weekend away?
- What else?

2. YOUR COMMUNITY'S 'HIDDEN CURRICULUM' CAN HELP FOSTER AN HOSPITABLE COMMUNITY

In a school, the 'hidden curriculum' is the informal lessons and values that the school's everyday life communicates to its students. It is unwritten, unofficial, and often unintended.

Your community has a similar 'hidden curriculum'. How intentional are you about it?

For example, does your 'hidden curriculum' express generous hospitality?

- Do members of the core team model how to make people feel they belong?
- Is the core team willing to listen actively to as much as the other person wants to share? And to go as deep in their relationships as the other person chooses?
- Are people made to feel special – for example, by celebrating exciting events and achievements in their lives?
- Do team members go beyond sympathy to patient empathy?

There are different degrees of hospitality.

3. THE FIRST IS A WELCOME INTO 'MY HOME'

It is equivalent to the invitation: 'Come into my home and share the meal I've prepared for you.'

Is that the kind of hospitality your new Christian community displays? You've listened to people, come up with an idea to love them, and community has formed round this loving activity.

Even though you've asked people to help you, basically it is your initiative. Hospitality is welcoming others into what you've developed.

Maybe this is unavoidable. Without your initiative, the new community would not exist. But it should be just a first step.

4. THE NEXT STEP IS TO TURN 'MY HOME' INTO 'YOUR HOME'

It's one thing to welcome people into your home where you set the rules, quite another to declare 'This is now your home.'

This deeper hospitality is how God welcomes us. In the Bible, in Genesis 2, God planted the garden, but then handed it over to Adam and Eve.

They were to care for it and develop it as they thought best. Apart from one rule (not to eat the forbidden fruit), they could create the rules. In effect, it became their garden.

Tim Mitchell started a new all-age community in England's East Midlands. He learnt that round him, for people under 40 a community was not 'their' community unless they could help lead it.

So from the start, he involved anyone who wanted to be involved in its leadership. Even agnostics and atheists could help prepare and lead the worship!

His was not a them-and-us community. Everyone could get involved.

Involvement deepens community.

Think of your community as a gift from God both to you and to the people the community serves. Let the gift go.

A gift is not a gift until it's released. Imagine you never handed over your presents at Christmas. How would they be gifts?

So let your community go. Release it into the hands of its members. Let it become real community by involving other people in leadership.

There's more.

5. THE GREATEST GIFT IS TURNING 'IT'S YOUR HOME' INTO 'IT'S GOD'S HOME'

When this happens, God becomes the host and community members God's guests.

In Luke 12.37 Jesus likens himself to a wealthy man who returns home. His servants expected to prepare him a meal, serve up, and clear away afterwards.

But the owner turns the tables. He cooks the meal, he waits on his staff, and he washes up at the end. The owner becomes the host to the people he employs, and waits upon them personally.

Jesus said, 'I no longer call you servants... but friends' (John 15.15).

Let your community be led by Jesus. Let him set the tone. Follow his example of serving his friends.

Encourage loving service to ripple through the community and shape its 'hidden curriculum'.

Suggest 'rhythms of life' that encourage community members to take their cue from Jesus in looking out for one another as good friends.

For example

- Members who wish might commit to pray (or have positive thoughts) for one other person in the community for a week. The next week they pray for someone else.
- Or they might agree once a month to invite at least one other member to a meal.
- Or through WhatsApp, they might swap skills and resources to help one another. ("Anyone got a lawn mower I can borrow?")

Community is a journey from 'my home', to 'your home', to 'God's home'. What stage have you reached?

DISCUSSION

Choose one or more of the following:

DISCUSS

Prayerfully discuss Acts 2.42-47 (the first Christians).

- What would the life of your new community look like if it was to share the characteristics described here?
- What would realistically have to change for your community to be more like the description in these verses, especially verses 44-47?
- What's the first thing you would change to move in that direction?

FORMING COMMUNITY

Discuss what forming community looks like in your initiative.

Ask:

- What do people do and say that indicates they have begun to belong?
- What are the signs that people are looking after each other?
- What routes into leadership exist?
- In the light of this discussion, what would you most like to change?

VISITOR

Invite a wise and experienced Christian to visit your community, and report back on the strengths and weaknesses they have observed. Might the visitor suggest how you could deepen your communal life? For example, might you and the visitor conduct a SWOT analysis:

- What are the strengths of our communal life?
- What are the weaknesses?
- What are the opportunities to deepen our communal life?
- What are the threats?

SHARE JESUS

12. EXPLORE FAITH

INTRODUCING PEOPLE TO JESUS

When they're trying to impact the world for good, many people go out of their way to love others and build community with them. But then they stall because they haven't helped people become followers of Jesus.

Listening, loving people and building community with them are great gifts from God, and they're what Christians ought to be doing.

But lots of people who aren't Christians do those things too.

There is one gift that God enables only Christians to offer. And that is life together with Jesus.

Only those that follow Jesus can offer this gift.

And it's a precious gift that gets to the heart of all things.

It's one thing to share some chocolates with a friend, but quite another to share your whole life with them.

So don't let your journey stop too soon. Find ways to share your life. And in doing so, share Jesus.

Keep going and don't give up! Help people in your new community talk to Jesus and explore what he says and does.

That way, what you're doing will combine his great commandment (to love others) with his great commission (to help people follow him).

1. YOU NEED A THEORY OF CHANGE!

The mission of Jesus was about abundant life – restoring people to health, forming a community of life-giving relationships, and promising a new society (God's kingdom) with wellbeing at its heart.

Jesus called his followers to make disciples so that this fuller life could spread across the entire planet (Matthew 28.19).

But often founders of new Christian communities don't know how to do this. They lack a "theory of change".

They do not understand how the Spirit can use their community to draw people into Jesus's richer life.

2. A THEORY OF CHANGE STARTS WITH A FRAMEWORK

The leaders of St Laurence, Reading, knew lots of young people with limited church background, but few were becoming Christians as part of a fuller life.

A senior church leader invited them to draw what they were trying to do. The diagram ended up like this.

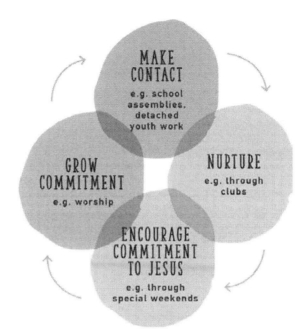

Making contact and nurture were working well, but the leaders weren't encouraging commitment to Jesus.

So they started special weekends.

Gradually from these emerged a worshipping community of nearly 50 young people, who grew in their commitment to Christ.

A framework enabled the leaders to see where they were going, filter out ideas that didn't fit, and spot the gaps.

For example, it was a big leap from clubs to the special weekends. Could they put in some smaller steps?

The loving-first cycle can offer this same sense of direction. You can use it to ask: 'What stage have we reached? What stops us going to the next stage? What are the opportunities?'

Listening, love and community create trust, and people must trust each other if they are to explore following Jesus together.

3. MAKE A BRIDGE BETWEEN 'COMMUNITY' AND 'SHARE JESUS'

Choose one or more of the following:

a. Start a distinct group for this purpose – perhaps a 'spirituality group'

You could explain, 'We'll discuss stories about Jesus, who is widely regarded as one of the world's greatest spiritual teachers, and see what we think of them.'

You can prepare the ground by introducing signposts to Jesus that spark spiritual conversations – see Chapter 13: Sharing good news.

In a language cafe, women from Sri Lanka met for tea and discussed topics in English. They were invited to pin prayer requests on a board. They began talking about their requests! Later, a group for people who wanted to know more about Jesus was formed.

b. Invite inquirers to the core team

Three families in Gloucester hosted a monthly Sunday breakfast for up to 60 people from nearby streets, and other activities such as ice cream and chocolate parties.

If asked, they talked about their faith.

Anyone showing an interest was invited to the core team, which met regularly over a meal to pray, plan and discuss the Bible. Visitors could come once or every time.

Within three years, the team had grown to 18 people and multiplied into two.

This is simple – just an invitation.

No need to fear questions like, 'Why did God allow that disaster?' You could reply, 'It's a question I struggle with, too. We sometimes talk about it in the team. Would you like to visit us next time?

'We eat together, have fun, do some planning, discuss stories about Jesus and pray in any way that makes us feel comfortable.

'No pressure! Join in as you like!'

c. Involve everyone

Eleven Alive met cafe-style in the morning and had a short act of worship at the end, geared for people who didn't come to church.

Periodically, after a shared lunch the whole community broke into four teams. Each team, led by a church member, prepared short worship for two sessions.

Importantly, anyone in the community – including agnostics and atheists – could join a team! This was highly fruitful in making disciples.

d. Do one-to-one Bible study with inquirers, then gradually connect them to each other in an explorers' group

Caution! Is the jump from 'community' to one of these options too big for your community? If so, can you put in some small steps to help people, if they wish, become more open to Jesus as part of your community's fuller life? See Chapter 13. Sharing good news.

4. SHARE STORIES ABOUT JESUS

In these different settings, you can invite inquirers to explore spirituality by looking at stories about Jesus and ones he told. Photocopy the story and read it through slowly, maybe two or three times.

a. Then ask these Discovery Bible Study questions:

- If the story happened today, what would it look like?
- What is it showing or telling me?
- Could it make a difference to my life? How?
- In the next session: Did it make a difference? How?

b. Or use these Deep Talk questions:

- What do you like best about the story?
- Where are you in the story?
- What would you like to change in the story?

c. Or ask these Bite, Chew, Savour and Digest questions:

These are based on *lectio divina* (a traditional Christian practice of scripture reading):

- What word, phrase or image in the story are you most drawn to today? (Bite)
- As you stay with your particular word, image or phrase, what else does it bring to mind? (Chew)
- Prayerfully wonder: why are you drawn to it? (Savour)
- How could it make a difference to your life? (Digest)

d. Or ask these kingdom questions:

- What's the passage saying that would make life more God-like?
- Where can we see signs of this God-like living round us?
- What could we do individually or as a group to increase this?
- In the next session: What have we done and what were the results?

e. Or mix-n-match the approaches

Or make up your own!

5. REMEMBER: YOU DON'T HAVE TO ANSWER THEIR QUESTIONS!

If someone asks a factual question, invite the group to google the answer.

If the question invites a reply that's a matter of opinion, ask the group: 'From what you know about Jesus so far, what do you think he would say?'

Don't worry if they get the 'wrong' answer. Our place in eternity does not depend on right answers.

For 1,800 years the church got the wrong answer about slavery. But this does not mean that St Augustine, Martin Luther and other heroes of the faith won't be in heaven. We're saved by faith, not by right answers.

So don't worry about the answers you hear. Focus on the priority, which is to help people learn the most important spiritual practice – the habit of relating their thoughts to Jesus.

Not feeling obliged to answer questions is an important principle. You are introducing Jesus in a way that leaves room for the Spirit and empowers the explorer.

Above all, be a good friend!

DISCUSSION

Choose one or more of the following:

DISCUSS

Prayerfully discuss Luke 13.6–9 (the story of the fruitless fig tree).

- If Jesus was to tell this story in your context today, how might he tell it?
- What is the story saying to you?
- What fruit might Jesus see in your initiative? And what more fruit might he be looking for?
- To encourage your community to bear this additional fruit, what would you have to do to 'dig round the tree and fertilise it' (verse 8)?

HELPFUL?

How helpful is the loving-first cycle for your 'theory of change'? What path through the cycle do you envisage:

- A separate inquirers' group?
- Inviting inquirers to the core team?
- Encouraging the whole community to move toward Christ together?
- One-to-one exploratory Bible study with inquirers?

THE HOW QUESTION

How will you explore Jesus within this path?

- Discovery Bible Study?
- Deep Talk Bible study?
- Lectio divina?

- Kingdom questions?
- A combination or some other way?

IDEAS

Discuss how you can best encourage people to follow Jesus.

- What would be signs that someone is following Jesus in your context?
- What are you already doing to encourage people to follow Jesus?
- What pleases you about this?
- What more could you do?

(Stuck for ideas? Consult Chapter 13: Sharing good news.)

VISIT AND REPORT

Think about visiting a new Christian community that has begun to draw people into faith. Report back to your team/ core group and discuss what lessons you can learn.

13. SHARING GOOD NEWS

SIMPLE AND NATURAL

The word evangelism puts a lot of people off. It conjures up a picture of Christians trying to make other people believe the same as them.

But how Jesus did evangelism was not like that. He didn't pressurise people. He just opened their eyes to possibilities.

Evangelism shouldn't be about selling Christianity. It's about helping people to see that they might have more choices than they realised.

When you share Jesus with people, you're giving them the chance to explore following him if they want to.

It's like showing people a whole new aisle of stuff in the supermarket that they'd never seen before. And the best thing is that it's all totally free, and really good for you.

Evangelism done well is never manipulative. That would be the opposite of offering choices.

To be a good evangelist is to invite people to embrace good news. People can accept the invitation or reject it. The choice is theirs.

1. EVER DISCOVERED A REALLY GOOD DEAL?

You have to share it with your friends!

Following Jesus is a bit like that. 'Evangelism' (from a Greek word meaning 'good news') is about joining in God's generosity.

It's about passing on God's fuller life to those who want it.

So, as part of the richness of your community's life, if people want to explore faith of course you will help them to do so, just as you would tell your friend about a really good offer.

2. BUT DO THIS CONSIDERATELY

Just as a new skill is taught step by step at the learner's pace, be sensitive to where people are in their journeys to faith.

Ask whether people have moved:

- From distrust to indifference – 'the community is OK, but I'm not interested in Jesus'
- From indifference to curiosity – 'Jesus seems interesting.'
- From curiosity to openness – 'maybe Jesus is for me'
- From openness to active seeking – 'I want to explore following Jesus'

- From seeking to joining – 'I want to follow Jesus.'
- From joining to growing – 'how can I live more like Jesus?'

You can't expect someone to jump from 'distrusting' to 'joining' in one leap! So to help people who are interested, put in small steps from one milestone to the next.

Caution! Remember that it is up to the person and the Holy Spirit whether they journey toward Christ. So relax, love the person for who they are, hold them in prayer, invite them to take another step if they wish, but above all keep valuing them if they choose to stay at a particular stage. No pressure!

3. FOR PEOPLE AT THE DISTRUST MILESTONE

Keep loving them. Be a faithful friend. Give them space. Let them learn to trust you. And listen to them. They know things you don't.

4. FOR PEOPLE AT THE INDIFFERENT MILESTONE

What would spark their curiosity? Use this KISS acronym to explore some possibilities:

a. Kindness. Suggest your community engages in acts of kindness

For example:

- Support an agreed charity
- Re-decorate a hostel for homeless people
- Invite members to declutter their homes and give away what they don't need
- Help people celebrate. One person introduced 'wrap presents at Christmas' for fathers and sons, with mince pies and mulled wine or juice. She included a five-minute talk about what Christmas meant to her

Let simple generosity provoke the response, 'Why are you doing this?'

b. Issues. Discuss issues from personal life

Here are three examples:

- One community gathered round the theme of 'fit lives'. Christians with compelling stories shared how Jesus was helping them to live a fit life.
- Another discussed Nooma DVDs about issues of life, treated from a light-touch Christian angle (go to YouTube or buy Nooma DVDs online).
- A third asked, 'What significant event has happened for you since we last met?'

Or discuss stories or themes from popular culture, such as:

- Films/TV programmes
- Song lyrics
- A book or article
- Celebrities in the news
- Computer games
- Sporting stories
- A significant political event

Questions might include:

- How did you react?
- What values were involved?
- Has anything like that happened to you?
- How would you have behaved in that situation?
- If God exists, what would he/she/it think about this?

Or interview someone from the community in your main event.

- Ask about a significant event in their life
- Or ask what they thought about a recent news story, or a new film, or the latest episode in a TV series
- Use some of the questions in the paragraph above, including the God question
- Then invite others in the community to discuss what they think

Or include in your main activity a short thought-for-the-day on 'How to live a fuller life'. Get loads of ideas by reading Richard Rohr's free *Daily Meditations*, on the Centre for Action and Contemplation website (easily Googled).

c. Start-up worship

This can be a step toward Christian worship for people who only half believe, are confused, or have only a faint awareness of God.

Choose symbols that:

- Resonate with people's concerns
- Connect these concerns to God ('as we each understand God') or to 'something bigger than us'
- Create a hunger for more

SPACE, a monthly 'cafe with a bit more', offered:

- A quiet space to think, meditate or pray
- A children's space with Bible-based activities
- A common space for everyone to enjoy a coffee, bacon roll, and chat

d. Spirituality. Possibilities include:

- A mindfulness group. Mindfulness is a simple form of meditation that encourages people to observe their thoughts and feelings without criticism – to be compassionate with themselves. It can lead naturally to reflection on spiritual themes
- Baby massage and prayer
- Prayer requests. Invite people to share these with one another or the core team, and to report answers to prayers
- One group invited people to download a walking route, discover small boxes of meditations en route, and use these to 'see beyond the view' and perhaps become curious about God. See: seebeyondtheview.org

A next step might be: 'Jesus is known as one of the world's greatest spiritual teachers. Shall we look at some of the stories he told and see if we agree with them?'

5. FOR PEOPLE AT THE CURIOSITY MILESTONE

a. Introduce an opportunity to explore Jesus, as described in 12. Explore faith/Guide:

- A separate explorers group
- An invitation to the core team
- The whole community explores together
- One-to-ones 'looking at stories about Jesus and seeing what we think of them'

b. Connect the opportunity to what interests people

- A group of men sought to improve the physical environment where they lived. In the pub afterwards, they discussed how they could improve other aspects of their lives, e.g. as fathers and at work
- Adam is gathering a community of classic car enthusiasts. He is exploring whether the theme of restoration might be a bridge to something with more explicit Christian content.
- For parents, invite them to explore answers to difficult

questions their children might ask, drawing on stories of the spiritual teacher Jesus.

- For people looking for hope, explore the following gospel stories:

Hope amid the storms of life: Matthew 14.22–33
Hope in a broken world: Luke 5.17–26
Hope for social outcasts: Luke 7.36–50
Hope instead of worry: Luke 12.22–34
Hope for those who feel lost: Luke 15.11–32
Hope for unpopular people: Luke 19.1–10
Hope at the point of death: Luke 23.32–43
Hope for those who are despised: John 4.4–18, 25–42
Hope for those who feel judged: John 8.3–11
Hope when you've been wronged: Matthew 18.21–35

c. Turn faith sharing into a simple invitation

Say someone asks, 'Where is God in that natural disaster?'

Reply honestly: 'I'm not good at explaining this stuff. But if you want to know why some of us still believe in God despite all this suffering, why don't you try the spirituality group that meets on Tuesdays?' Or 'Come along to our core group.'

6. FOR PEOPLE AT THE OPENNESS MILESTONE

Discuss stories about Jesus using one of the approaches described in Chapter 12. Explore faith:

- Discovery Bible study
- Deep talk
- Bite, chew, savour and digest
- Kingdom questions

These are brilliant approaches because:

- Scripture does the evangelising.
- Christians can talk about their faith naturally.
- The studies are easy to lead – hardly any preparation!

7. FOR PEOPLE AT THE SEEKING MILESTONE

a. Keep going with the Bible study!

Allow time.

b. Remember: you do not have to answer difficult questions

Invite people to Google answers to factual questions.

For questions of opinion, reply: 'From what you know about Jesus so far, what do you think he would say?'

Keep encouraging different views to be expressed and affirming people's right to disagree. Do not let Christians shout down someone who knows less about Jesus than they do.

Let encouragement be your motto (1 Thessalonians 5.14).

c. Don't let people become dependent on you

Empower them and leave room for the Spirit! Encourage them to:

- Trust the Bible
- Find out more about it
- Learn from one another
- Develop a Christ-centered way of thinking

8. ABOVE ALL, BE A PATIENT FRIEND!

Stay loyal to the person whether they choose Jesus or not.

Remember: some people inch to faith. Others make a sudden decision. Each journey differs.

So respect people's uniqueness, pray, trust the Spirit, and keep asking not 'What would have worked for me?' but 'What would work for them?'

DISCUSSION

Choose one or more of the following:

READ

Prayerfully read Luke 5.1–11 (The calling of the first disciples). Think of people in your community.

- Who is washing their nets (v. 2) – so busy with life that they scarcely notice Jesus
- Who has let Jesus into their boat (v. 3) – they are listening to Jesus, but with no personal commitment to him?
- Who is putting into deep water but with skepticism (v. 4–5) – they are starting to respond to Jesus, but have yet to be convinced?
- Who is falling at Jesus' knees (v. 8) – ready to follow him?
- Who are Simon's astonished companions (v. 9) – captivated, but not yet ready to fall at Jesus' knees?

MILESTONES

Use the milestones to faith above, or your own version.

- Who is at which milestone?
- What signposts would help people take another step?
- What will you do to put in the appropriate signpost?

BIBLE STUDIES

Work through some of the Bible studies in Section 5 (b).

- You could do this as a team/core group over a series of meetings. Or in an explorers' group. Or in one-to-one Bible study with an inquirer.

- Why not use one of the four approaches mentioned in the Guide and unpacked in 12. Explore faith / Guide?
- Find a time to review what you've done. What have you found helpful? In what ways, if any, does the approach you used need adapting?

ASK FRIENDS

Ask some friends who don't go to church what they think would be attractive about following Jesus?

- What things come out top?
- What's the most important thing they don't mention?
- What are the implications for how you share Jesus?

RESERVATIONS

Ask some friends who don't go to church what stops them following Jesus.

- What things come out top?
- In what ways do you sympathise with these reservations?
- What might you do and say to commend Jesus in a manner that addresses these reservations?

CHURCH

14. GROW DISCIPLES

HOW TO ENCOURAGE CHRISTIAN MATURITY

If you want to help new Christians grow in their faith, beware of telling them what to do.

A young couple who'd just become Christians were on a Christian basics course. After two sessions, they stormed out. 'Last week you told us to come to church every week. Now you've told us to stop sleeping together. You're just like everyone else. You only want us to join you on your terms.'

The people running the course meant well, but their timing and approach derailed the couple on their journey towards Christ.

Jesus taught in an invitational way. When someone asked him whether a woman caught in adultery should be stoned to death, he said: 'let the person who has never done wrong throw the first stone.'

His hearers had to work out for themselves how this applied to them – and it's worth noting that no one threw any stones.

Spiritual maturity doesn't lie in following rules, but in owning faith – in making it yours from head to toe. So by all means give new Christians support. But also encourage them to explore – and trust the Spirit to grow their faith.

1. HOW CAN WE BEST DISCIPLE NEW CHRISTIANS?

The priority is not to pass on Christian beliefs, such as those in the creeds. Jesus didn't focus on teaching people theoretical doctrine. He concentrated on people's behaviour and relationships. He repeatedly called his followers to love their enemies, forgive 70 times 7, turn the other cheek, and more.

Jesus was interested in understanding that grew faith and led people into lives of healing, justice and wholeness.

The first Christians emphasised practice, too. They theorised about their beliefs as they worked out what it meant to follow Jesus in everyday life.

So follow their example. Encourage mature Christian behaviour. Focus on the four overlapping sets of relationships that are at the heart of the Christian life (see Chapter 11. Church?).

2. DIRECT RELATIONSHIPS WITH GOD

Encourage prayer to become an everyday habit, as it was for Jesus.

For example, invite community members to exchange prayer requests on social media, swap prayers for each other, and report answers to prayer. Text them regular prayer prompts.

Keep studying Scripture and ring the changes. See Chapter 7. Explore faith for ideas.

In Birmingham, leaders of B1 invited adults to read a Bible passage in advance and discuss it with their children. When the community met, individuals in age-based groups shared what they had learnt.

This became a way of encouraging families to worship God on their own and then together.

3. RELATIONSHIPS WITH THE OUTSIDE WORLD

Develop communal practices (or 'rhythms of life') – things you do together to follow Jesus in everyday life.

Adopt a contemporary version of the 18th century Wesleyan 'bands': suggest people support each other for a limited period in practicing a certain behaviour.

For example

- For 6 weeks, each person does one act of generosity a week and shares with the group how they got on.
- As a form of prayer, one group writes protest letters on behalf of Amnesty International (as Just Church did during its worship); another group writes on behalf of a different organisation.
- Three or four people contract for a period to eat more healthily, or to read an evening Bible story to their children.
- During Lent, individuals agree to do one act of kindness a day and share with each other what they've done.

People could do this in self-selecting groups or as a whole community.

The support of other Christians makes a huge difference. As St. John of the Cross said, in community the individual becomes a stone that others turn into a sculpture.

4. RELATIONSHIPS WITH THE WIDER CHURCH

Christians are baptised into the whole Christian family, and discipleship involves learning from and contributing to it.

So encourage your community to:

- Link up with a local church or congregation and join in social, learning, missional and worship events – e.g. a family fun day, a series of study evenings, or celebrating Easter together. Start with social or educational events. Often it's easier!
- Attend a Christian festival or conference.
- Download Christian resources from the internet.
- Worship regularly as a community and in another congregation you're connected to.

5. RELATIONSHIPS WITHIN THE NEW CHRISTIAN COMMUNITY

Encourage conversations about the difference Jesus makes to everyday life.

People learn by asking questions, putting into their own words what they've learnt, trying out ideas, and listening to other people's comments.

Jesus did not merely preach at people. He asked questions and left room for dialogue (e.g. Mark 8.27–30; 10.17–31; John 6.25–59). So allow plenty of time for discussion.

If you have used one of the Bible study approaches in Chapter 12, 'Explore faith', you may want to ring the changes.

For example

> Invite someone to download a relevant podcast or video and share what they have learnt.
>
> Or invite a person in advance to consult one website with expert information about the passage and someone else to look at another. Each shares their findings.
>
> Look for material produced by someone whose ministry is well recognized by the wider church. Recorded sermons by a well-known preacher might be a possibility.

This way the group takes responsibility for becoming more informed in its study.

6. DON'T LET THE GROUP BECOME DEPENDENT ON YOU

If someone asks a factual question, don't feel you have to answer it. Suggest they Google the information instead, and ask if they think the source is reliable.

If the question invites an opinion, throw the question back to the group: 'From what you know about Jesus so far, what do you think he would say?'

Invite prayerful silence while people consider their responses. Then invite them to share what they think God has been saying to them.

Encourage them to listen rather than correct one another.

Remind them that the church is full of different viewpoints. Indeed, it could be said that the church's history is one long argument!

If we listen to different views carefully, however much we disagree with them, we may get a fresh glimpse of Jesus.

'It takes the whole church to reveal the whole Christ.'

So encourage people to listen to each other, be patient with one another, and then share what they've learnt about Jesus through their listening.

Help them develop a Jesus-centered habit of thinking.

Let them rely prayerfully on the Holy Spirit to speak through the Bible, the group and the wider church.

Paul was eager that the Corinthians build one another up in the faith (1 Corinthians 14.5, 12, 26). This was the responsibility of the whole congregation, gathered around Scripture.

7. HERE, THEN, IS A WAY TO SAFEGUARD AGAINST ERROR

These four sets of relationships – with God directly, with the world, with the wider church and within the new Christian community – are all centred on Jesus. They provide boundaries within which to explore faith and discover God's will.

The relationships balance each other. Together, they stretch personal faith and behaviour. They encourage people to become well-rounded believers.

DISCUSSION

Choose one or more of the following:

DISCUSS

Prayerfully discuss Hebrews 5.11–14. What practical steps might help your community – or the community you envisage – grow beyond infancy?

KEY VALUES

Discuss what are key values for your community. Then for each value, figure out one practice that would express that value.

For example, if one value was hospitality, a practice might be to find a 'buy one and get one free' offer, and give the free item to someone else.

Or the practice could be sitting next to or spending time with someone you find difficult in the community.

Try these practices in the team/core group, and then spread them out to others in the community.

REFLECT

Reflect on what you have read in this chapter about helping new Christians to grow in their faith.

- What are the good things your community is doing about this and where is it falling short?
- What might you do differently that would help new Christians mature in their faith?
- How does the prospect of doing these things differently make you feel?

DISTINCTIVES

What does it mean to live a distinctive Christian life in your context? i.e. what specific practices would express a Christian way of life in your setting? For example:

- If your community is based on a common interest or sport like soccer, what would it mean to be a Christian soccer player?
- If your community is drawn from a particular locality, such as an apartment block, what would it mean to be a Christian in this apartment block?
- If your community is drawn from a particular demographic, such as teenagers, what would it mean to be a Christian teenager in the school(s) the young people attend?
- How might you encourage those who've recently come to faith or are journeying toward faith to explore these practices?

ONE NEW THING

Think about what you have seen, heard and read in this unit. What one new thing to nurture Christian faith do you think you should introduce?

- If this new focus became a reality, what would members of your community see, hear and feel?
- What would make you most pleased about their response?

15. CHURCH EMERGES

BECOMING A CHRISTIAN COMMUNITY

What happens when someone becomes a Christian because of a friendship from work, or the gym or the food bank?

Often, their Christian friend invites them to go to church somewhere else because there isn't a church at work, in the gym or in the food bank. So they have to be extracted from their context to attend church.

In the Bible, in Mark 5, Jesus cured a man who was literally being haunted by his demons. The man was totally freed.

Then he thought he would have to leave his home to follow Jesus.

But Jesus told him to stay put, tell his family and friends what had happened, and maybe... just maybe... grow a group of Christ's followers right there.

New Christians don't need to join a congregation elsewhere. A new Christian community can take shape in the very place where they come to faith.

In a familiar place, new Christians can start to follow Jesus and worship him with people they already know. As they do so, 'Church' will emerge naturally around them.

1. SO GIVE THEM THE TOOLS

Equip people to grow their own version of 'church'. Don't pass on your ready-made church.

When Jesus returned to heaven, he did not leave his followers with a blueprint for church. They didn't have:

- The name for church
- Adequate leadership structures (see Acts 6. 1–7)
- Set words for Christian worship

Jesus had told them to make disciples, baptise people and break bread together. That was all.

Prayerfully drawing on his teachings and led by the Spirit, his followers made up the details as they went along.

Jesus left behind not a Lego church but the Lego bricks.

So copy Jesus. Help new believers discover for themselves, led by the Spirit, what being a Christian community means in their context.

2. START BY SHARING LEADERSHIP

Do this from the very beginning. Work with the people you are called to serve. Don't start something for them.

Involve them at the design stage. Welcome their ideas and contributions. Bring them into the decision-making.

As people journey to faith:

- Empower them to lead Bible and other discussions as soon as possible
- When they have questions, ask them to imagine how Jesus would respond, drawing on what they know about him
- Point them to Christian resources online
- Teach them to rely on Scripture, the Spirit, the wider church and each other, not you

3. INTRODUCE WORSHIP

a. Encourage prayer

Invite the community silently to:

- Become aware of God's presence
- Review with gratitude what's happened since the community last met
- Pay attention to their feelings
- Choose something that's happened since they last met and pray from it
- Look toward tomorrow
- Share anything they would like with the wider group

b. You do not need a conventional sermon!

Jesus didn't only preach. Much of his teaching occurred through discussion – e.g. Matthew 16.13–20; 19.16–30.

1 Corinthians 14.26 assumes lots of participation in the process of Christian learning.

So keep going with discussions that have begun to centre on Jesus. These may become your 'sermons'.

Break the gathering into small groups to do an activity – for example:

- Write a blog or tweet about a Bible passage
- Imagine describing what they've learnt to a friend
- Take photos to illustrate what the passage is saying
- Silently reflect on the passage
- Listen to a podcast

c. Include other elements of worship

Consult websites such as Proost (proost.co.uk)

d. Experiment!

In Cook@Chapel, Katherine invited teenagers to write thank you prayers, put them into a cooking bowl, draw out a prayer and read it.

When next time she forgot the bowl, the young people asked, 'Where is it?' She knew the experiment had worked.

Likewise, when she introduced a lighted candle, one of the group spontaneously turned down the lights. The group was taking ownership.

e. Teach the principles of worship

For example, explain the spiritual reality check provided by confession during worship and how this aids spiritual growth.

Describe some ways Christians have practised confession:

- Written confessions
- Being accountable to each other for one's behaviour, as in early Methodism
- Writing down thoughts, actions or attitudes you want God to change and burning the papers as a prayer offering

Ask the group, 'What would work best for us?' and experiment with their ideas.

Remember: what's worked for you may not work for them.

For background to elements of worship, read (from an Anglican perspective) Mark Earey & Gilly Myers (eds), *Common Worship*

Today: An Illustrated Guide to Common Worship (HarperCollins, 2001). It's got loads of information that might interest other denominations as well.

4. WHAT ABOUT BAPTISM AND HOLY COMMUNION?

To be fully church, a new Christian community will want to baptise new believers and break bread together.

So what happens if the community is led by lay people and is part of a church in which only ordained ministers can baptise or preside at Communion?

There are several possibilities:

- Ask the local minister to baptise or preside at Communion as a representative of the whole church.
- Periodically join the original congregation in celebrating Communion.
- Hold an agape meal (or 'love feast' or 'remembrance of the Last Supper'), involving a meal, Scripture, prayer, sharing stories, listening to or singing hymns/songs, and sharing bread and wine, but without using set words. To avoid confusion, explain that this is not Holy Communion as normally celebrated in your denomination.
- Combine these possibilities – e.g. attend a nearby church occasionally and hold 'love feasts' in between.

5. CONNECT TO THE WIDER CHURCH!

When new believers are joined to Christ, they become spiritually related to everyone else in his family.

These connections must take concrete form if they are to mean something for those involved.

So form a 'mixed economy' or 'blended' church. If you're part of a local church:

- Begin by sharing social activities. Involve your community in arranging them. Members will feel more part of the whole if they give as well as receive.
- When people are ready, join in worship, outreach, and study groups.
- Make sure your community is represented in the church's governance.
- Join your parent congregation in attending Christian events elsewhere – a festival or conference, perhaps.

Involvement in the wider church is great for spiritual growth and necessary to be part of the Christian family.

Caution! Church is much more than worship and connecting to other Christians, of course. Chapter 11. Church? will help you become a well-rounded Christian community.

DISCUSSION

Choose one or more of the following:

DISCUSS

Prayerfully discuss Luke 9.1–6 (Jesus shares his leadership).

- What do you like best about this story?
- Where are you in it?
- What makes you feel comfortable and uncomfortable?
- What are the lessons for leadership in your new Christian community (or for the one you are beginning to imagine)?

ON MISSION

It has been said that the best way to grow in faith is to be on mission, in your everyday life, in community with other Christians. How far do you agree with this and for what reasons? If you do agree, what are the implications for members of your community?

CHANGE

In the light of what you have read in this chapter, what would you like to change in your community?

- How would you explain this to others in the community?
- Who else would agree with you, and what practical steps might they take to support you?
- How might you make it easier for others to come on board?

LEADERS

Picture or list the people regularly involved in your community.

- Who is already exercising some form of leadership? Might they be stretched further?
- Who else might you encourage to exercise some leadership? How?
- What support do you provide for your (emerging) leaders? Could you improve it?

WORSHIP

Look through a service of Holy Communion.

- List some of the ingredients – the welcome, prayers, etc.
- Ask what ingredients are missing from your worship.
- Is there one of these ingredients that you might add to your worship for a period?
- How might you introduce it and encourage the community to make it their own?

PARENT CHURCH

What connections does your community have to your parent church or other local churches, your denomination or network of churches, or to the worldwide church?

- How might you strengthen these connections or develop some further ones?
- Does your parent church, denomination, or network have particular gifts and characteristics that you would like to see expressed in your new community? How might you foster these?
- Are there characteristics you wish to avoid?!

16. CHURCH?

ARE WE AUTHENTIC CHURCH?

Whether you call yourselves a church, a congregation, a community, or something else is not that important.

What matters more is the question 'Is your group part of God's family?'

When you hear the word 'church' you may think of a building. But the Bible talks about the people of God being like living stones that make up the church, with Jesus as its cornerstone.

In other places it pictures the church being more like a flock of sheep than a building.

The church is the people of God. Do members your group see themselves as part of God's people?

Being God's people is our human destiny. The last pages of the Bible picture a new city where God will live with us forever. He will dwell in the midst of his people.

No Christian community is perfect, but each is called to be a foretaste of that destiny and to point others to it. It's a challenging call but well worth pursuing.

So why not live the future today? Whether you call yourselves a 'church' or not, live out your destiny and become the people of God

1. MANY PEOPLE FIND THE CHURCH OFF-PUTTING

It often feels formal, hierarchical, and distant from everyday life.

We live in a relational world – people are constantly on their mobile phones! Yet for many people, the church does not seem focused on healthy relationships.

Which is a tragedy.

2. RELATIONSHIPS ARE THE VERY ESSENCE OF THE CHURCH

Many descriptions of the church in the New Testament have relationships at their heart. For example:

- The household of God (1 Timothy 3.15).
- The body of Christ (Romans 12.5).
- The vine and the branches (John 15.5).

Any church, whether a new Christian community or otherwise, has four overlapping sets of relationships, all centered on Jesus:

- With God directly in prayer, worship and study.
- With the wider church.
- With the outside world, and
- Within the community itself.

The church at Corinth, for example:

- Experienced God directly (1 Corinthians 12.7–11).
- Connected to other Christian communities – members read Paul's letters and looked up to people in the church at large (1 Corinthians 1.12).
- Engaged with the outside world (1 Corinthians 14.23–25).
- Interacted relationally in worship (1 Corinthians 14.26–31).

3. THESE FOUR SETS OF RELATIONSHIPS ARE EQUALLY IMPORTANT

That's because Jesus is central to each of them, and together they make for a balanced and healthy community.

Throughout history, these four sets of relationships have always been central to the church.

They have been expressed in a multitude of ways, but the one Spirit has worked through this variety.

So if your new Christian community looks rather novel, don't worry! It can still be an authentic expression of the people of God.

Just look for ways to grow these four sets of relationships. Once all four are present, your community will be paddling in the shallow end of the church.

4. WHERE DO BIBLE, SACRAMENTS AND LEADERSHIP FIT IN?

Christians have traditionally seen these as being fundamental to the church.

You can think about this by distinguishing between the essence of the church and what is essential for the church.

The two need not be the same. A referee is essential for a soccer match, but is not the essence of the game. In the West a knife and fork are essential for eating, but are not the essence of the meal.

The four sets of relationships are the essence of church, while baptism and Holy Communion, the Bible, and recognised leadership are essential for the church.

Scripture, sacraments, and leadership originated in the church's relationships. They arose from interactions within the community that Jesus founded.

And the Holy Spirit works through them to build up the church's relationships.

Other forms of worship, social events, outreach activities, organisational arrangements, discipline, and so on, all have a similar purpose.

They encourage, support, and strengthen the community's four overlapping sets of relationships – with God directly, the world, the wider church, and within the community itself.

5. SO KEEP MOVING FROM THE SHALLOW TO THE DEEPER END OF CHURCH

Make sure baptism and Holy Communion, the Bible, and recognised leadership are present in an appropriate form. Surround them with other life-giving rhythms and practices.

Keep asking: "How well do our practices nourish each of the community's four sets of relationships? Are our worship, Bible study, organisation, and other practices deepening these relationships?"

If not, make changes. Prayerfully shape everything you do to best enable each of these relationships to flourish.

That way, your community will become – as suggested earlier – the people of God.

6. HOW DO YOU KNOW WHEN YOUR COMMUNITY HAS 'ARRIVED'?

How can you recognise that it has become a congregation (or the equivalent) of a local church, or even a local church in its own right?

Some signs are:

- When it begins to grow into the four overlapping sets of relationships that comprise the church, and
- When you are introducing what is essential for these relationships to flourish

7. WHEN YOUR COMMUNITY LOOKS LIKE GOD'S PEOPLE, TREAT IT AS SUCH!

New Testament Christian communities were both connected to the wider church and had appropriate autonomy.

So, ask the following questions:

1. How far has your community grown healthy relationships of accountability and mutual support with your parent and other churches? What are the strengths and weaknesses of these relationships? What more could you do to strengthen them?

2. How far has your community traveled toward being an expression of church? Is it paddling in the shallow end of church or is it wading toward the deeper end? Has the time come for it to receive greater official recognition?

3. If you are already linked with a local church, denomination, or network of churches, is your community appropriately represented in their decision-making? If so, how well

is this working? Has the time come for more effective representation?

4. Does the community have appropriate autonomy? In particular, how much freedom does it have in appointing its leaders, including the overall leader? Is there a shared understanding by all involved, and is this written down somewhere?

5. Will the community be protected when the leadership of the parent church/denomination or network changes? For example, could a new minister close you down if they wanted? What say will you have in appointing a new minister?

6. Who should you consult about any of this, and when?

8. DO YOU WANT SUPPORT IN YOUR JOURNEY TO BECOMING CHURCH?

If so, get together with others traveling in the same direction.

Meet regularly to share stories, learn (that's what disciples do), and encourage each other. As you do this, you will be experiencing church in yet another way.

You will be engaging:

- With God directly through prayer and study.
- With the wider church through Christians drawn from different contexts.
- With the world as you learn from stories of how others do mission.
- With one another in the learning community itself.

DISCUSSION

Choose one or more of the following:

DISCUSS

Prayerfully discuss Acts 11.19–30.

- Imagine that the Jerusalem Christians were an existing church today and the church in Antioch was a new Christian community. Retell the story as if it happened today.
- What does the story tell us about blended church'?
- What one thing will you do differently as a result?

PARENT CHURCH

Perhaps with someone wise and prayerful from the wider church, review your new community's relationships with your parent church and the church beyond. Use the questions in Section 7 above.

IMPORTANT DECISIONS

When you personally/as a core team/as a community make important decisions:

- Which set of the church's relationships do you tend to take most note of?
- Could you pay more attention to the other relationships?
- If so, what would you be doing differently?

EVALUATE

Evaluate how well your team/core group or your new community is growing in its fundamental relationships.

a) Select one of the following sets of relationships:

- With God directly in prayer, study, and worship
- With the world
- With the wider church
- Within the fellowship

b) Ask yourselves:

- Over the past few months or year, in what specific ways have we seen growth in this set of relationships?
- Over the next few months or year, what further growth would we like to see?
- What are we doing now that helps us to move in this direction?
- What else would move us in that direction?

c) Consider a review process:

To discern how the Spirit has led you recently and wants to lead you in the months ahead, you might plan to review each of the four sets of relationships in this way once a year. When would you do this?

REPEAT

17. DO IT AGAIN!

BE SUSTAINABLE BY MULTIPLYING

If you're trying to grow a new Christian community, how will you know when you've succeeded?

Some people think a proper church lasts for decades. So success would be about being durable.

But think of the very first church in Jerusalem. In terms of history, its life was miniscule. The church ended less than 40 years after it started, when the Romans destroyed Jerusalem in AD 70.

Yet it was one of the most fruitful churches in history. Its members started new Christian communities in Judea, Samaria, Cyprus, Antioch and all over the place. They gave birth to the worldwide church that's still growing now.

Look at today's churches. Some have lasted a very long time, but are they all still thriving?

Churches can keep going for decades, but keeping going doesn't necessarily make them fruitful.

If you want to see fruit don't aim for durability, pray for reproduction.

Help new Christians to copy the first followers of Jesus and to grow new Christian communities themselves.

1. FOUR REASONS TO REPRODUCE YOUR COMMUNITY

a. A shift from solid to fluid society

The past saw fewer changes than today. Now, change is everywhere and the world is in constant flux.

In this more fluid world, we must expect new Christian communities to often be fluid too.

Changes in personal circumstances may force some key people to leave a new community. Or the community may run out of steam because key members start a family, peak in their careers, or care for elderly relatives.

The community comes to the end of its natural life.

However, if your community started a new one, it would live on in the life of its offspring. It would endure despite life's ebbs and flows.

b. A shift from durability to generativity

In this fluid world, sustainability need not equal a long-lasting community. Such a view was appropriate when life was more stable. But our fluid society requires that we re-imagine sustainability.

Our prime goal should be to start not a sustainable community, but a fruitful one (John 15.1–8). Fruitfulness will include birthing further communities.

Remember the Jerusalem church? Despite its short life, it was highly fruitful. It birthed – generated – countless new Christian communities.

A lesson for us?

c. A shift from making disciples in church to making them in life

Traditionally, we have relied on the church to make disciples – on worship, courses, and small groups.

These are great for drawing you into God's story and learning the principles of Christian behaviour.

But often they are less good at relating faith to everyday life.

You might think: 'How does "turn the other cheek" apply to my bullying boss? If only I could discuss this with another Christian who understood the situation.'

That's why finding a Christian friend and discovering how to love people round you is so important. It creates opportunities to learn together what following Jesus means in that context.

Starting a new Christian community in life speeds growth in spiritual maturity. That's because...

Community requires us to:

- Trust God
- Find practical ways to love other people
- Contribute to a Christian team
- Find natural, loving, and relevant ways to share the good news
- Connect faith to everyday experience.

How better to mature spiritually than to be on mission, in your everyday life, with other Christians!

So encourage new believers to find a friend, start a new Christian community, and grow spiritually.

d. A shift from growing a congregation to multiplying congregations

Often communities expand, then plateau. Starting another community can offset this levelling off.

A woman formed a Christian community in her front room with people from a poor neighbourhood. Space became tight. So they moved to a nearby school.

Big mistake!

The larger gathering made the original members feel less involved and put them off leading. They drifted away.

Might multiplying small groups within the neighbourhood have been a better approach?

2. THREE STEPS

a. Raise expectations

Expectations are the seed of new life. So, from the beginning, pray that your community will reproduce. Make this a long-term goal. And talk about it!

Don't say to yourself and others, 'I feel called to start a new Christian community.' Say, 'I feel called to start a network of new communities.'

Language shapes thought. So use the right language. This will shape your expectations. And your expectations will shape everyone else's.

When people in your community ask about faith, explain that starting a small Christian community can be part of a 21st century Christian life.

If they are intrigued, tell them some of the stories in the book by Michael Beck and Michael Moynagh, *The 21st Century Christian: Following Jesus where life happens.*

Encourage inquirers to follow Christ with the possibility of starting a Christian community in mind.

b. Find an apprentice

From an early stage, look for one or two people who could start the next community. They may be in your core Christian group or among those coming to faith.

Keep praying for them. Invest time in them. Nurture their faith. When they are ready, share your vision of a network of Christian communities. Use *The 21st Century Christian* with them. In particular, let them take you into their worlds. Ask questions to stimulate their thinking. Use Chapter 7, 'Starting', as a prompt.

Challenge others in the community. There may be more potential apprentices than you realise.

c. Keep things simple

Introduce people to Jesus by using approaches they can easily copy.

For example:

- Show DVDs they can share with their friends
- Use Bible study methods they can easily adapt – see Chapter 12, 'Explore faith'
- Find ways of praying that they can share with others

This is why you have to be intentional. If you're praying your community will reproduce, adopt reproducible practices that become answers to your prayers!

3. TWO EXAMPLES

These stories are told in the free app, FX Godsend, section G) REPEAT, Unit 17 'Do it again', in the videos section.

a. Thirst

Parents and carers near Cambridge came to faith through Thirst, a discussion group among people who were dropping off their children at school.

They were so enthusiastic they wanted to invite their friends and children. But their friends were at work and their children at school.

So they started Thirst Too on Saturday afternoons – an all-age community for the people they knew.

b. Sorted

Sorted began among 11 to 14-year-olds. As the group got older they asked their leaders, 'Why don't we do with the next generation what you did with us?' And they did!

4. ONE CHALLENGE

Remember God promised Abraham descendants as numerous as the stars (Genesis 15.5)? But he hadn't even got one child! Imagine how he felt.

Maybe the idea of reproducing makes you feel like that. 'How can I think about multiplying my community when I haven't even begun?'

Be like Abraham. Trust God.

And try this thought experiment.

Imagine a cafe-based community holds 'spirituality sessions' for the cafe's customers.

Several come to faith.

New believers meet with the Christian core for Bible study, prayer, worship, and fellowship. Their faith deepens.

But the community is small. A couple of the founders move away. Energy evaporates. The community dies.

Here's another possibility. Though small, the community flourishes by reproducing.

- Perhaps the founder starts a further community, while staying in touch with the original one.
- Or the community sends out a small team to start another community in the same context.
- Or someone just beginning to explore Jesus teams up with another Christian to start a different-looking community in another context – and then someone else does the same, and so on.

The original community comes to the end of its natural life, but it lives on through several offspring.

Which will be your future?

DISCUSSION

Choose one or more of the following:

READ ACTS

Prayerfully read Acts 11.19–23. (You may have read these verses as part of the Bible study in 15. Church? where the focus was on 'blended' church. Here the focus is on 'doing it again'.)

Before discussing the passage, ask whether reproducing the church mean reproducing similar or different-looking communities?

Re-read Acts 11.19–23. Discuss:

- What is each of us getting out of the passage?
- What are the lessons for our community?
- What could we do next?

SIMPLICITY

If you are at an early stage in starting a new community, consider how you can keep things simple so that they can be easily used and adapted by those coming to faith.

- How will your community be organised so that new Christians think they can do something similar?
- What will you do to invite people to faith in a way that new Christians can easily copy?
- How will you make prayer, study, and worship easy for new Christians to share with other people they know?

PRAYER

Review the prayer life of your core team and/or your community.

- What are the most common topics of prayer?
- How often does starting further communities feature?
- What would have to happen for this to be a more frequent topic?

IDENTIFY

In your community, who might be in a position to help start another Christian community?

- What are they saying and doing that encourages you to reach this conclusion?
- What are you already doing to encourage, equip, and support them?
- What else might you do?

IMAGINE

Imagine during the night a miracle happened and your new community began to give birth to further communities.

- If 10 represents the day after the miracle and 1 is furthest away from the miracle that you could be, at what number would your community be now?
- If your community was to move 1 point up the scale, what would it be doing differently?
- What steps would you have to take to move to this next point?

APPENDIX

The contents of this book are also available online, and can be accessed at:

fxresourcing.org/godsend

For those who are participating in the Church of England's Greenhouse initiative, the contents can also be found at:

churchsupporthub.org/fxgreenhouse

Godsend is also presented in an app format which you can download by searching for 'fx godsend' in the App Store or Google Play.

If you are involved with a Messy Church or another form of inter-generational church, you can access supplementary material by visiting:

fxresourcing.org/godsend/messy-church

We're grateful to the God For All team in Cumbria who have created a Study Guide with ideas for using Godsend in a group setting. They've given us permission to make it available here:

fxresourcing.org/godsend/study-guide